# IN THE LIGHT
# OF THE TRINITY

Statue in Trinity College Garden—Bl. Julie Billiart

TRANSLATED BY SISTER HELEN MADELEINE, S.N.D.

# IN THE LIGHT
# OF THE TRINITY

The Spirituality of Blessed Julie Billiart
Foundress of the Sisters of Notre Dame de Namur

by François Charmot, S.J.

74389

*with Foreword by*
His Eminence Richard Cardinal Cushing

BX9
4485.3
.B5
B533

The Newman Press · Westminster, Maryland
1964

The present volume is a translation of the French edition, *Dans la Lumiere de la Trinite*, published by Desclee de Brouwer.

*Nihil obstat:*  
    THOMAS J. RILEY  
    *Censor librorum*

*Imprimatur:*  
    RICHARD CARDINAL CUSHING  
    *Archbishop of Boston*  
    June 30, 1962

*O Blessed Trinity, Father, Son,*
*Holy Spirit, Be Praised Forever*

# Foreword

One of the most convincing arguments for the holiness of the Church is the outstanding holiness of so many of its members. Among those who bear witness of the enduring power of God's grace are the founders and foundresses of religious communities. That there are so many of them, each pointing out a particular pattern of striving for religious perfection, makes it all the more evident that Christ our Lord, Who Himself laid the foundations of the religious life, has likewise endowed it with divine efficacy for the service of the Church. Each religious community, so different from all the others, finds nevertheless its inspiration and its exemplary causality in Him Who was God as well as man.

The Sisters of Notre Dame de Namur have become well known throughout the Christian world not only for their skill as educators, but especially for their consistent fidelity to the ideals of their foundress, Blessed Julie Billiart. The forthcoming canonization of this extraordinary servant of God will draw attention to the program of spirituality which she formulated for her daughters in religion. As we follow this program in the detailed analysis of Father Charmot, S.J., so capably translated by Sister Helen Madeleine, we are impressed on the one hand by its depth and scope, and on the other hand by its clarity and simplicity. Thousands of Sisters of Notre Dame de Namur have meditated faithfully on Blessed Julie Billiart's teachings, handed down to them over the years as the starting point for their own advance towards religious perfection. As they have met the problems of their religious lives and dedicated themselves to the work of their Institute, they have manifested unmistakably, beneath and beyond their individual differences, that characteristic spirit which has identified them as Blessed Julie Billiart's daughters, and sanctified their personal lives with Blessed Julie Billiart's devotion and supernatural courage.

Those who read this book will easily recognize the source of the qualities which they have found in the Sisters of Notre Dame de Namur. They will find, moreover, some suggestion of the secret of the happiness which Blessed Julie Billiart's daughters have so consistently radiated, and which is responsible in no small measure for the large numbers of vocations which have found their way into the novitiates of the Sisters of Notre Dame de Namur. Every one who knows and loves the Sisters will want to read this interesting account of the material and spiritual growth of their Institute. I congratulate Sister Helen Madeleine for having made the book available at a time when it will be of such great significance and productive of so much good.

RICHARD CARDINAL CUSHING
*Archbishop of Boston*

# Preface

Julie Billiart, Foundress of the Sisters of Notre Dame, was formed spiritually by eminent priests: Abbé Dangicourt, who instructed her in Holy Scripture; Pere Thomas, former Doctor of the Sorbonne; Pere Varin, of the Fathers of the Faith; Pere Enfantin, her spiritual director.

But Julie was specially enlightened, directed, strengthened by the Holy Spirit, in a deluge of precious graces which theology calls "gifts of the Holy Spirit."

Julie was born in 1751, at Cuvilly, a small village of Picardy. From early childhood she experienced suffering and the trials of illness. Slowly paralysis made its inroads in her, until at the age of thirty-one she was completely disabled. But nothing could prevent this docile soul from heeding the inspirations of the Holy Spirit, from acquiring the supernatural fruitfulness which distinguished her in the eyes of the world as one who perpetuated the Redemption of Christ.

To penetrate the secret recesses of this soul, one must follow Saint Paul and the magnificent Pauline revelations concerning the Father, the Son, and the Holy Spirit, as well as the profound devotion of St. Ignatius to the Trinity. "From these sources came the spirituality of Julie Billiart; from these, too, her Congregation imbibed and still imbibes its sanctity, and the ardent zeal to which her daughters are called."

# The Life of Blessed Julie Billiart

On July 12, 1751, there was born in Cuvilly, a small village in Picardy, the fifth of the seven children of Francois Billiart and of Marie Antoinette De Braine. She was baptized that same day and was given the names of Marie Rose Julie.

Her parents supported their family by a small-wares shop and by farming. These courageous Christian parents soon mourned the loss of four children and confided to God the future of the others.

Robust, intelligent, alert, sensible, and conscious of the love of God even from her earliest years, Julie undertook to help her parents by her rapid progress in school and by her cheerfulness and devotedness at home. When she was only eight years old, during recreation she took on the role of teacher of catechism and of Sacred Scripture, and the children of her own age, and even older ones, listened enraptured.

Discerning this precocity the holy Curé of Cuvilly taught his little parishioner who loved to talk *about* the good God, how to speak *to* Him. As soon as she was nine years old, he permitted her secretly to receive Holy Communion. Daily Julie offered her little victories over self to Jesus, made frequent visits to Him in the Tabernacle, and, under the direction of Madame de Séchelles, she went to make Him known and to console the poor and the sick.

In spite of their meager income, the Billiarts were a happy family. But repeated losses brought about real financial pressure which thieves transformed into misery. When Julie was sixteen years old, she had to earn her living. She was obliged to work, to join the harvesters. Profiting by this contact with them, she reminded them of their duties as Christians.

Intrepid, and above all, strong in her trust in God, for seven years she went on foot, sometimes on horseback, even during the night, to sell in the shops the stock which had been left behind in her father's shop by the robbers.

One evening while she was in conversation with her father in the old store, a shot came through the window pane. Julie's nerves were shaken so badly that her walking and her bodily movements were impaired.

How discouraging to be immobilized at twenty-three years! But no! Julie organized her life under that persistent malady: she taught catechism; she visited the sick with the aid of crutches, and even spent nights beside their beds. When she was thirty-one the paralysis became complete, and Julie prepared for a holocaust. She had the privilege of daily Communion. For long hours she conversed with Jesus, absolutely oblivious of what went on around her, absorbed. A light touch would bring her out of this state. She would smile, then welcome her noble benefactors, Madame de Pont l'Abbé and Madame Baudoin, whose counsel and support she would be. So, too, she would receive her pupils for catechism. Moreover, the valiant cripple, suffering in her entire body, worked with her hands. Years passed. Five times she was the victim of illnesses so severe that death seemed imminent.

Then came the Revolution, and with it the Civil Constitution for the Clergy. She withstood the schismatic priest in her parish and organized resistance against him. Some fanatics wanted to burn her alive in the chateau where Madame de Pont l'Abbé was hiding her. She escaped from their fury only by fleeing to Compiégne, hidden in a cartload of straw.

It was a cold winter night when she arrived at the courtyard of an inn where the driver of the cart abandoned her. She could hardly swallow the drops of wine which her sixteen year old niece, Felicité, put between her lips, as they waited for daylight to seek a lodging.

In her new environment she suffered much from the privation of all religious help, from the impossibility of carrying on her catechism classes, and from the necessity of changing her dwelling five times in three and one-half years.

In spite of her suffering Julie made lace for a living. She clung to God whose Presence she no longer felt. One Good Friday, however, in her little room, there appeared before her a great luminous crucifix, surrounded by a multitude of women in an unfamiliar religious costume. From the Vision came a voice: "Behold the Daughters whom I shall give to you in an Institute which shall be marked by the Cross."

How would that be done? Behold Julie with Felicité at Amiens, in a room rented from Madame Baudoin at the Hotel Blin. The first stake in the construction of her Congregation was about to be put in place. Mlle. Francoise Blin de Bourdon, daughter of one of the noblest families of France, was presented to Julie, who was unable to speak at that time. The first interview was not agreeable to Mlle.

Blin. Inspired by charity, however, the noble Viscountess returned from time to time to the bedside of the invalid in whom she soon discovered a precious guide for her spiritual life. The ties grew so strong that Julie and Francoise were separated henceforth neither in mind nor in heart, in spite of all that conspired to sever this union. The humble Viscountess allocated her entire fortune to Julie's apostolate and proclaimed her always the *only* Foundress of the Sisters of Notre Dame.

As her speech improved, the invalid gathered around her bed a group of ladies. Christian charity was their object, but that same charity, spotted by the hostile power, made a new exit imperative: this time to Bettencourt, not far from Amiens.

The resurrection of this village to a true Christian life by means of the cripple Julie and her companions convinced Pere Varin of Julie's real vocation. When she returned to Amiens in 1803 she opened an orphanage and welcomed helpers. A vow of chastity, together with that of a particular care for the instruction of youth, was pronounced by the courageous paralytic, by Francoise Blin, and by Catherine Duchatel, on February 2, 1804. They took the name of Sisters of Notre Dame, and acclaimed Julie as their Mother.

Her reputation as a catechist was well known: other Institutes in Amiens sent her their pupils, many of them. When, during the missions, the arches of the Cathedral resounded with the preaching of the Fathers of the Faith (the Jesuits of that era) the humble cripple, in a portable chair, explained with her companions the sermons to the women and children, for whom the sermons were too deep. Crowds came. What a pity that such an apostle should be

a paralytic! That should be no obstacle, decided Pere Enfantin, a man of strong faith. He obtained her cure by
means of a novena to the Sacred Heart.

Then, after a retreat of thanksgiving and of organization,
the paralytic, then fifty-three years of age, travelled on foot
and horseback, with great diligence, alone or with postulants, in all sorts of weather, as far as Flanders. These trips
were justified by apostolic necessities, new foundations, and
the recruiting of subjects.

But Mere Julie took no time out for rest. When she
arrived at her destination, she at once took up the business
at hand, sought audiences with bishops, dealt with land-
lords and officials, drew up plans, proposed improvements.

All divine works must be marked with the seal of the
Cross: And so the Foundress, her Congregation, the first
Sisters were well acquainted with difficulties, humiliations,
reproaches, and to a certain degree with persecution; calumnies, destined to deprive Mere Julie of the confidence
of bishops and of the Sisters, were spread abroad in various
places, and led the Bishop of Amiens to expel her from his
diocese.

Monseigneur Pisani de la Gaude offered her generous
hospitality at Namur. In 1807 his episcopal city received
the exiled Sisters and became the seat of their Motherhouse.
Since then the Daughters of Blessed Julie have been known
as the Sisters of Notre Dame *of Namur.*

On February second, at the words, *Lumen ad revelationem gentium,* Julie was rapt in ecstasy. The first Sisters
said that it was shown to her at that time that her Sisters
would one day cross the ocean.

The number of her subjects multiplied; so, too, new

foundations. But in January, 1816, Julie became seriously ill and had to abandon her work plans. For several weeks she suffered intensely, but to those who sympathized with her she replied, "God is our good Father; He is so good, the good God!"

During the evening of Palm Sunday her condition became worse. Recalling the graces which the Lord had granted her, she gently began to sing the *Magnificat*. A little later she lost the power of speech, and in the early hours of the following morning, April 8, she gave up her soul to God, fearful neither for herself nor for her work.

At Namur only one rumor was heard, "The Saint is dead!" Many people came to venerate the precious remains and to honor the humble Servant of God.

In 1906, Holy Church honored Julie Billiart by admitting her to the number of the Blessed. Today her Daughters are rejoicing that the Church will place her soon in the number of the saints.

# Contents

# Introduction

God is admirable in His Saints!

We repeat this again, as we learn to know better the life and the works of Blessed Julie Billiart, Foundress of the Sisters of Notre Dame.

These pages are only the echo of the deep repercussions produced in us by this holy, suffering, and fruitful life.

A poor country girl, intelligent but deprived of the means of instruction which many other saints had, a pure soul, submissive to divine grace, Julie Billiart was formed spiritually by eminent priests: Abbé Dangicourt, who gave her lessons in Holy Scripture; Abbé Thomas, Doctor of the Sorbonne; Pere Varin, Superior General of the Fathers of the Faith; Pere Enfantin, her spiritual director, etc. Above all, she was enlightened, directed, and strengthened by the Holy Spirit.

The Holy Trinity heaped upon her graces which theology calls the *Gifts of the Holy Spirit*.

From her childhood, she was chosen by Jesus Crucified to bear special testimony: serious and continual sufferings, even paralysis, which did not prevent this soul, so docile to the Holy Spirit, from having a supernatural influence and fruitfulness which made the perpetuity of the Redemption of Christ sparkle in the eyes of the world.

Before we begin a detailed analysis of her virtues, we can readily apply to Julie Billiart the profound utterance of a theologian, the term, "Victim of the Trinity." He said:

A Victim of the Trinity is a soul of deep faith who, disregarding all visible things, has fixed her dwelling in God, in the company of the Three Divine Persons, dwelling with Them, *in the very Life of Light,* love, and joy.

In the light of her faith everything in the history of the world and in the events of her own life appears to her as a manifestation of that Divine Will, which even in the least details of the world carries out the eternal designs of God.

She knows that the Cross is the supreme grace of our conformity to Christ, and that throughout the nights of the Church Militant there is a luminous flight of souls seeking the immutable and beatifying Trinity.

Such is the makeup, broadly depicted, of Blessed Julie, who, from suffering to the exalted contemplation of the Trinity in everything, raised herself, by repeated assaults of the Cross and by grace, to a high sanctity, and who had strength "in her weakness" to found an important Congregation of religious educators.

To penetrate into the soul of Blessed Julie Billiart by the surest means, to find the principal source whence her Congregation took its beginnings and *the eminent sanctity and the ardent zeal* to which her daughters are called, one should study the spirituality of Saint Paul and of Saint Ignatius.

When one examines the spirituality of Saint Paul or Saint Ignatius, one is convinced that both began their apostolic life by devotion to the Holy Trinity. All authors who have studied the spiritual ascent of Saint Ignatius have disclosed his many visions of the Trinity, his extraordinary devotion to the Father, and to the Son, and to the Holy Spirit, and the gift of abundant tears which he shed whenever he turned to the Trinity in prayer. In his spiritual diary occur constantly his prayers to the Three Persons considered individually, in the unity of the Divine Majesty.

From that contemplation filled "with loving glances," he drew, one may say without exaggeration, his *Spiritual Exercises,* his Society, and his Constitutions.

Saint Paul, who loved Jesus Christ passionately, as did Saint Ignatius and others later, contemplated Him not only in His life on earth, but in His glorious life at the right Hand of the Father.

We should cite here, for example, the beginning of the Epistle to the Ephesians, which will guide us in our search for the supernatural lights with which the spirituality of Blessed Julie Billiart is filled. "Blessed be the God and Father of Our Lord Jesus Christ who has blessed us with every spiritual blessing on high with Christ!"

The following continues to praise God the Father for His Infinite Goodness:

Thus He has chosen us in him before the foundation of the world, that we should be holy and without blemish in his sight, in love. He predestined us to be adopted through Jesus Christ as His Sons, according to the purpose of his will, unto the praise of the glory of his grace, with which he has favored us in his beloved Son (Eph. 1:4–6).

What, then, are those blessings in Christ? They are the union, and even the unity, of all and everything in Christ. It has been possible only by the Cross, by the Blood, by the Purification, by the Redemption.

Said Saint Paul:

In him we have redemption through his blood, the remission of sins, according to the riches of his grace. This grace has abounded beyond measure in us in all wisdom and prudence, so that he may make known to us the mystery of his Will according to his good pleasure. And this his good pleasure he purposed in him to be dispensed in the fullness of the times: to re-establish all things in Christ, both those in the heavens, and those on the earth (Eph. 1:7–10).

In this Mystical Body under one Head, however, Saint Paul sees diverse vocations. This remark is important to recall that the graces of God are not the same for all, but different according to the vocation of each religious order. He reverts to it several times, for example, in Ephesians 1:5–6: "He predestined us to be adopted through Jesus Christ as his sons, according to the purpose of his Will unto the praise of the glory of his grace, with which he has favored us in his beloved Son.

Finally Saint Paul puts all his trust in the Holy Spirit: "And in him you, too, when you had heard the word of truth, the good news of your salvation, and believed in it, were sealed with the Holy Spirit of the promise, who is the pledge of our heritage for a redemption of possession, for the praise of his glory" (Eph. 1:13–14).

The spirituality of Blessed Julie Billiart and of her Congregation is the putting into practice of the magnificent Pauline revelations concerning the Father, the Son, and the Holy Spirit. And that is the basic reason why she seems to us so exalted, so profound.

We shall consider her sanctity first in her relationship with the Father, then with the Son, finally with the Holy Spirit. Thus we shall see better what a wealth of graces flows from the characters imprinted on her virtues by each of the Three Divine Persons.

*"We have come to know, and have believed the love that God has in our behalf"* (I JOHN 4:16).

# 1 Daughter of the Father

Blessed Julie attributed everything, creation, the mysteries of Christianity, all the blessings and all the trials of life to the goodness of God.

To say that God is good, is to say not only that He is by nature a Father, that He is, as Saint John said, Love, but also that this paternity from all Eternity begot a Son, consubstantial with Him, to whom He gave all that He was, except the character which distinguished Him as a Person, and that in His Son He has loved us to the point of making us adopted sons, His well beloved children, eternal co-heirs with the Incarnate Word.

Goodness equals love, but emphasizes the infinite need of giving life and all else.

That is why Blessed Julie Billiart loved to speak continually not only of the fatherhood of God, but of his goodness. She made this divine goodness her motto, her continual thought, the breath of her soul.

Ah! how good is the good God! . . . Often say these burning words to the souls with whom you deal. That is the perfect apostolate, an apostolate dear to Infinite Love which desires witnesses, missionaries, apostles.

Let us repeat with love: God is good . . . Oh! How good is God! With Saint Bruno let us say to God Himself: "Oh! Divine Goodness! Always and everywhere, all for the love of God!

I know more and more how much one should trust the Lord in all things. Ah! How good is the good God! How good it is to put all our trust in Him! Oh! yes! yes! yes!

Think of the care the good God has taken of us always, even before we turned to Him with our whole heart. What will He not do for you today when you desire to serve Him without reserve. Will He who did so much to save us, will He ever refuse us His holy grace? Oh! no, no, provided that we have confidence in Him. He gives us a thousand more graces than we deserve. The eyes of the Lord are fixed on us as those of a good Father. Yes, the good God is our good Father; it is on this solid foundation we should lean. He assures us that even though a mother may forget her child, He will never forget us.

Words such as these Blessed Julie had constantly in her heart and on her lips. Frequently she borrowed her maxims from the Holy Scripture. One may say that truly few souls have resembled the Psalmist more in praising the goodness of God.

Psalm 106: "Give glory to the Lord, for He is good, for His mercy endureth forever."

Psalm 107: "Give thanks to the Lord, for He is good, for His love endureth forever. . . .

Let the mercies of the Lord give glory to him, and his wonderful works to the children of men. . . .

Let them sacrifice the sacrifice of praise: and declare his works with joy! . . .

Who is wise, and will keep these things, and will understand the mercies of the Lord?

Psalm 117. Give praise to the Lord, for he is good: for his mercy endureth forever.

Let Israel now say that he is good: that his mercy endureth forever.

Let the house of Aaron now say that his mercy endureth forever. Let them that fear the Lord now say, that his mercy endureth forever.

A hundred other passages in the Psalms, which all dedicated persons, priests and religious sing fervently every day, repeat under different tones in biblical terms the word which vibrated unceasingly in the soul of Mere Julie.[1]

Why all this homage to the goodness of God, if it is not because more than the other perfections that our intelligence sees in Him, that of goodness is, according to the revelation of the Old and of the New Testament, first, universal, constant, deep.

Recalling the thought of Tertullian, and without exaggeration that of all the Fathers, Bossuet expresses himself thus:

God began His works by an outpouring of His Goodness over all His creatures. His first inclination is to do us good.

[1] Perhaps it is due to her initiative that the Sisters of Notre Dame inserted in the first *Manual of Prayers* (1840) thirty Psalms to arouse confidence.

And, in truth . . . in order to understand well what is the first of these inclinations, one must choose what is found most natural inasmuch as nature is the root of all the rest. Then, has our God anything more natural than this inclination to enrich us by the profusion of His graces? As a spring sends forth its waters naturally, as the sun sends out its rays naturally, so God does good naturally. As He is good by His nature, courteous, and infinitely rich, He must by nature be also beneficent, liberal, noble.

May I be pardoned for prolonging this citation. For the motto of Blessed Julie, by which we have yet to develop the depth of the sense that she had of goodness in her spirituality, has its foundation in Scripture.

The *scriptural* basis has been magnificently explained in the encyclical of Pius XII, entitled *Haurietis aquas,* on the cult and the devotion to the Sacred Heart.

The *theological* basis is found in the work of Saint Thomas and in those of all the schools. Bossuet sums up their thought:

When God punishes you, O impious one, the reason is not in Him! He wishes that no one should perish. It is your malice, it is your ingratitude which bring down His wrath upon you. On the contrary, if we want to incline Him to bless us, it is not necessary to seek far for motives; His own goodness, His nature, in itself so beneficent, is a cogent reason which never ceases. That is why Tertullian said emphatically and to the point: *"goodness is first because it is according to nature,* and *severity follows because it is a cause."* As if he said: There is no reason for the divine munificence, if one may speak of it as such; it is the very nature of God. Only severity seeks causes and reasons; but it does seek them and we give them . . . Consequently, as Tertullian said so well: that God is good is due to His own nature; that He is just is due to our nature. The exercise of goodness is sovereignly voluntary in God; that of severity, forced; the former proceeds entirely from within; the latter from an alien cause. So it is evident that whatever is natural, interior, voluntary, precedes always whatever is external and forces.[1]

Blessed Julie had a very special grace to live these consoling truths in the very midst of Jansenism. But today, when Jansenism has recoiled and struggles in a kind of agony, the Congregation which she founded should believe that it has a major role to play in spreading a spirituality which has for an unchangeable foundation the motto: "How good is the good God!" We live in a time when Christians of every type repeat as a password: God is Love. But it is far more necessary that the souls who hear it and say it believe it truly as they believe in the love of a fiancé, or in that of a father or a mother, or in that of an inseparable friend. There is an abyss between the faith of certain Christians who speak much about the love of God but who do not live their faith, and the faith of Julie Billiart who proclaimed the goodness of God as the bird sings, as the fire warms, as the clock sounds, that is to say, as the spontaneous expression of her whole being. Some, in truth, practice their religion under the dominion of fear, of anxiety, of anguish, of depression. They know that God is Love. On occasion they say so. It is like the refrain of a song. But when the song is ended, they are recaptured by the bitter prose of everyday life. When God is no longer Love, He becomes judge, or an indifferent spectator of our maladies. Others have a more real understanding of the goodness

[1] Bossuet, *Sermon sur la bonte et la rigueur de Dieu*, II, 138.

of God. They recite the *Our Father* as they speak to their earthly father, with the conviction that God listens to them tenderly. But their faith is limited almost to a rite. For it is alive only in the strict observance of the exercises of piety. When they do not pray, when they are not in church, or when suffering does not cause them to call God to their assistance, then the Father in Heaven, they think, is no longer busy about their concerns but about His own.

The third class of Christians is that of the Sisters and Daughters of Blessed Julie Billiart, and before her, of a great number of Saints to whom God has been revealed as a Father. These souls privileged by grace do not distinguish the days or the hours when God shows His love for them, as Holy Scripture says; but they are persuaded that He loves them every moment of the day and of the night, in all things spiritual and in those which are material, in all that may happen to them. They have not faith in love in the abstract, but in the continuous web of existence. What is true for all that is not God, to know the ephemeral, the transitory, the unforeseen, the past, and the future, is not true for the goodness of God. Like His very Being, it is immutable, living, eternally beneficent. These souls breathe the goodness of God, as their being breathes the air, without which they would stifle. They have not the too human views of the first who make of God an image like to man. They see with evidence, through faith in the Scripture, that God is good or He is not; if He ceases to be good, He ceases to be. That is impossible. God, who has no need to receive, since He is the infinite plenitude of being, has one only need, to love. That is the paradox of love. Because He has the plenitude of being, His love hastens to share His life, His blessedness, His perfection in His Word, as a Father, and with the Three Persons with His adopted Sons. He must love His creatures; with Him it is a need—the only need—of Infinite Love.

Others express the same idea under the form of a thirst, although God cannot thirst for anything, except for His Spirit, which is God. The thirst for God which the poor man or the sinner experiences, is not the thirst, so to speak, of God for man which precedes it; it is the principle of all thirst, of every desire, of every yearning of creatures for God. "God's thirst for man," writes a theologian, is the most astounding reality there can be.[1]

When we shall speak of Jesus, known, adored, loved, imitated, glorified by Blessed Julie Billiart, we shall refer more completely to the goodness of the Father in the mystery of the Incarnation. But as this mystery is conceived, desired, created eternally by the Father in the Trinity, we must recall here the words of Saint John: *"God so loved the world that He gave His only begotten Son,"* that the world which believed in Him (then in His Fatherhood of Love) may not perish, but may have eternal life (that is to say, His own life). For God has not sent His Son into the world to condemn the world, but that "the world may be saved by Him." And he who believes in the goodness of God does not imagine that the Son is only a prophet, a messenger, a doctor, a revealer. For the Father, to be good is everything. Faith in goodness consists in being fully assured that nothing, nothing that is human, that interests man's world, is irrelevant to God. In fact, God in Jesus has so loved the world that His personal humanity has taken over—from His

[1] *Vie chretienne* (Dec., 1958), p.9.

birth to His death and again in His Flesh and Blood in the Blessed Sacrament—not only all that is good in men, but what is evil, so that the union might be complete: our faults at first, then our sufferings, finally our death. Being without sin, He made Himself as a sinner for us: The Pauline expression includes all sin, all that man has known and will know of homicide and deicide. He did not take the innocent and the purified flesh of man but He clothed Himself with unpurified flesh that He might purify it, nay more, that He might divinize it. And this goodness would impress us less sensibly if it had not been shared with us in suffering. For we know sin only by faith; but suffering we know by concrete experience. Jesus thirsted for the sufferings of man. He wished, through love, to experience in His immaculate flesh agonies, flagellations, bondage, torture, scorn, nakedness, atrocities of all kinds, human griefs, mortal torture. Who knows the number of human sorrows, voluntarily experienced by Jesus? He thirsted ("With desire I have desired to eat this Pasch with you"), because He had the thirst of a man.

A chapter of the *Imitation of Jesus* will open up other perspectives. Beforehand we must try to understand how faith in the goodness of God is for Julie Billiart and for the Sisters of Notre Dame the foundation of a deep spirituality that one meets rarely in other Congregations.

All spiritual directors agree that eighty per cent of souls capable of leading a fervent Christian life would not be paralyzed by frequent temptations to discouragement if, in their relations with the Holy Trinity, they had established that essential truth which Julie Billiart acquired and was commissioned to spread abroad: the goodness of God.

Without doubt, this truth must not only be accepted by the mind, but it must enter into the daily life, as we found it constantly in the spirituality of Blessed Julie.

Immediately from this faith flows faith in the gratuitousness of the gifts of God, a gratuitousness so often recalled by Saint Paul. But another fact is that we are not worthy of any grace—this expresses the negative aspect of gratuitousness—as well as the conviction that there is nothing that one cannot expect of a God "so good," so "infinitely good," when we consider the positive aspect of this gratuitousness.

All Christians believe, with more or less true humility, that they have nothing which they not received from God through Jesus Christ, "that of themselves they are only error and sin." They must, however, through faith, repeat with Saint Paul: "God said to Moses: 'I will have mercy on whom I have mercy, and I will show pity . . .' So, then, he has mercy on whom he will, and whom he will he hardens" (Rom. 9:15–18). But this certitude, while emphasizing the truth of their nothingness, yet depresses them sometimes; they draw from it more discouragement than humble dependence.

Saints, like Blessed Julie, do not falter on such a good road. For them gratuitousness signifies also that "God the Father has blessed us by all sorts of spiritual blessings in Christ Jesus." So He has granted to them in abundance, unworthy though the recipients may be, almost infinite graces, particularly to the Virgin Mary by her preservation from original sin and the divine maternity; thus He has created the Angels in the splendor of grace; thus He has made Augustine, formerly a slave of impurity, a great Doctor of the Church; thus He made of Magdalen, the sinner, a Saint of Love and of the Resurrection; and many criminal souls specially gifted with grace, without any merit on their part, at the same time without any natural right, God loved and filled with His graces beyond all human measure. They believe with Saint Paul "that those whom He has foreknown, He has predestined also to become conformed to the image of His Son, so that He may be the eldest of a multitude of brothers; and those whom He has predestinated, He has called them also, He has justified them also; and those whom He has justified, He has also glorified." They believe that God will glorify them since He has justified them; God "who spared not His Son, but Who delivered Him up for us all," why would He not give us all consideration?

To me? Yes, to me, as to all, for the gift of God is for all, all sinners.

This faith in the gratuitousness of the goodness of God is very important. But it is necessary also to believe that this gratuitousness is without measure for all of us: "For I am sure that neither death, nor life, nor angels, nor principalities, nor things present, nor things to come, nor powers, nor height, nor depth, nor any other creature will be able to separate us from the love of God which is in Christ Jesus, our Lord" (Rom. 8:38–39).

For Blessed Julie gratuitousness was faith in the superabundant goodness of God. The Father has no reason to limit His favors towards His sons, since it is only goodness which inspires Him.

A spirituality founded on this faith is true, solid, deep, efficacious, and the conclusions which are drawn from it for sanctity are of an incomparable power.

From it comes directly the fact that confidence in the goodness of the Father animates the soul to carry out all the great designs of God.

The confidence of Julie is so fervent and so inviolable that it recalls at once that of Saint Ignatius and of Saint Francis Xavier, and in modern times, that of Saint Therese of the Child Jesus. One sees them all on the same height and all established in the same way, on that which is most deeply seated in God: His Goodness.

They must not be confused with the optimism of happy characters, nor with the sentimental piety of weak characters, weak in the face of trial, nor with the complacency of strong characters, accustomed to conquer obstacles.

Their confidence in God goes beyond the expectation of the possible and hopes, so to speak, for the creation of the impossible.

God is so inclined to enlist His creatures to share in His great works, that He makes possible what He "commands," what is beyond human strength, "the impossible."

It is in this spirit that Saints have governed their Congregations.

All will go well, my Daughter, because I put all my hope, all my confidence in the Lord. It is His work, not mine. And so I go through difficulties. One should fear nothing, but trust in the Lord. Let us leave all to the good God. He will draw us out of our difficulties, if it is His Will.

Let us note how aptly this holy soul recalls the goodness of God:

My good Daughters, our loving Saviour loves us so much. It seems to me that He has eyes only for all of us, for those especially who go to Him the most simply, who give Him the most marks of confidence; for, note well, it is to confidence that He grants most graces and His Love. The more you will show Him marks of confidence, the more He will love you. You will all have a great confidence in *this good and tender Father,* will you not?

In my prayer this morning I promised Our Lord that I would tell every one, my dear good Daughters especially, to have a great confidence in our *Good Father* in Heaven.

The eyes of the Lord are fixed on us as those of a *Good* Father. Yes, the good God is our *Good Father;* we must lean on this solid foundation . . . Let us leave all to the *Good God.*

Let us fear nothing: it is the *Good God* who will protect us. If the *Good God* is for us, who will be against us?

Men are only men; but the *Good God* is not like men. We must put all our confidence in the *Good God,* my good Daughter; you and I, we must do that from morning till night, and say to Him: "My God, it is Your work. My God, it is Your work. You know that we are poor and incapable of doing anything good."

We might quote long pages like these, in which the refrain of confidence in the goodness of God gives an original character to all that Blessed Julie has written. It is original, no doubt, but so like to the writings of the Saints, particularly of Saint Ignatius whom she venerated, and of Saint Therese of the Child Jesus. Born a century later Saint Therese has reproduced by the same inspiration many traits of Julie, particularly that of spiritual childhood. Julie's partiality to the virtue of simplicity is a forerunner of that which the modern Saint made so attractive in her "Little Way."

Though reaching back into the past, Julie's spirituality is notably Ignatian. In fact, are the following excerpts those

of Saint Ignatius or are they quoted from Blessed Julie?
One hesitates to say:

Infinite Goodness is sovereignly communicative of its benefits, and Eternal Love is more eager to give us sanctity than we
are to desire it.

We tire of receiving the gifts of God more quickly than He
tires of bestowing them upon us.

There are few persons, perhaps there is no one who can
understand perfectly how much we hinder God when He
wishes to work in us, and how much He would do in us, if we
did not prevent Him.

God can do more to save me than the whole world can do
to lose me, as the test of time will show.

Our confidence should be so strongly grounded in God that
at need, even without a boat, we would not hesitate to believe
that we could cross the ocean on a simple plank. He who
would do great things for God should take care to be very wise
and to consult his head and his hands, I mean his ability and
his personal resources. If the Apostles had followed such philosophy they, so few in number, so bereft of science, so helpless
exteriorly, would never have undertaken that great enterprise
so far above human power: the conversion of the universe, the
conquest for Christ of the princes and savants of the world by
means of a cross.

Saint Ignatius and Julie, faithful to the Gospel (Matt.
6:25–35) and to Saint Paul, proclaimed with one voice
that there is no other foundation (I Cor. 3) than He who
has been proposed: Jesus Christ.

But to make more definite the character of this confidence found in her spirituality, one must distinguish confidence in the Love of the Father and confidence in His
providential action. For the former is general and unites

persons: man and the Trinity; the latter is particular and unites the actions of those Persons. They are not distinguished by their origin which is the overflowing Goodness of God, but only by their effects. The first expects from Love the sanctity of man; the second the collaboration of the adopted Son of God. Both enable us to benefit by the charity of the Trinitarian life.

It is clear, consequently, that the spirituality of an Active Order should have its foundation in a total confidence in the Goodness and in the Providence of God.

This confidence is called by a special name: "Abandonment to Providence." Although a long treatise would be necessary to deal with this subject adequately, we should, however, recall the principles and their consequences. For not to show that Blessed Julie Billiart wished throughout her life to be the instrument of Providence would be to misunderstand her soul and the general program in her great Congregation.

All Christians speak of Providence as of a superhuman government in the history of the world. But very few make of this dogma a powerful, purifying, and consoling means for the strengthening of their faith and for the increase of their charity. If we had to attribute to the divine government only exterior and interior events, material and spiritual things which please us and which make life easy and happy, perhaps everyone would thank Providence for its continual benevolence. But faith in Providence is not limited to the temporal well-being of individuals and of nations. It constrains us to believe, as the Vatican Council said, that "God, by His Providence sustains and governs the universality of the beings He has created, reaching out mightily, from one end of the earth to the other, and disposing all with sweetness. All things are clear and undisguised in His eyes, even actions yet to be performed which proceed from the free will of creatures.[1]

It is clear that wherever there is being, however lowly it may be, the Infinite Cause of that being is present and active, giving it existence and the continuity of existence in time. God is then everywhere—and in the most hidden recesses of matter and of spirit; but wherever there is being God is there also—not partially, for He is indivisible—but entirely, with His Intelligence, His Love, His Will, His Omnipotence, with all His infinite resources. He uses them for the greatest good of beings, according to His Wisdom. Not a hair of my head can fall without the permission of the Heavenly Father; and it is the same for all animals and for the elements of created Nature. Everything, absolutely everything, is part of His plan.

These thoughts have a wonderful spiritual value in the case at hand. That is why they recur so frequently in the Old and in the New Testament.

To give an exact idea of their value, one must add, that neither freedom, nor evil, nor our sins, nor unforeseen accidents, nor our illnesses, nor our death, nothing that we think, experience, or do, is free from this absolutely universal power of Providence.

There is in this faith, since it is as vital as self-love or maternal love, that wherewith to raise ourselves to an extraordinary union with the Holy Trinity. Blessed Julie had

[1] D.B., n. 1784: "All things which He created, God in His providence guards and governs, reaching from end to end mightily, and ordering all things sweetly" (cf. Sap. 8:1).

no need to read the enormous documents of Scripture proofs, Fathers, theologians, and historians on which this faith is solidly founded. The light of the Holy Spirit alone sufficed to give her a supernatural point of view concerning the Providential Goodness of God in all things, that all the Doctors of the Church together, if they are only savants, do not acquire.

Let us not insist on traditional documentation, for we are not writing an abstract treatise, but let us consider the remarkable spiritual heights which faith attained in the soul of Julie.

One may reduce them to four complementary perfections: total abandonment, serenity, simplicity, childlikeness of heart. When these perfections are raised to the degree to which Blessed Julie practiced them, it is not difficult to perceive the power of her supernatural radiation.

*Abandonment* was frequently the subject of her conferences and of her letters, because she knew its abundant and stimulating fruits.

Divine Providence will regulate my little concerns, or rather those of the good God, for as for myself, I have only to do what the good God shows me, moment by moment. I wish only to go from day to day doing the holy Will of God, entirely abandoned to our good and adorable Master in all that He wills. Fiat . . . Fiat . . . That is the goal of my peace, I desire no other.

Oh! How good God is. He has permitted that I be deprived of all sorts of help: God only is necessary for His work, I leave all in His Hands.

It is true, then, that I can never say: I shall do such or such a thing at such or such a time. Oh! no, no! Mine must be a continual Fiat . . . , and yours, too, my dear Daughters.

Surely when there is question of analyzing the nature and the extent of abandonment, there is no lack of fine pages in the great spiritual writers, depicting the importance of this virtue in spirituality.[1] But Blessed Julie, by her personal experience, confirms the most enlightened ideas:

Abandonment consists in giving oneself to the good God, moment by moment, letting oneself be guided by Him, without stirring under His paternal Hand. It permits neither anxious misgiving, nor regrets, nor fear, nor desire.

One is impressed to see in her notes the unity of her thoughts, which the majority of writers do not have. Her soul sees the "good God" always and in everything. For her, Providence is paternal.

Abandonment recognizes and adores the paternity of God. One must let oneself be guided by the *good God*. He is so good, that He can wish for nothing but *good* for our greater good and for His greater glory. The *good* God does not wish that we go more quickly than He does. We have enough for the present moment; let us leave the rest in the bosom of the *good God, our tender Father.* All will go well if we let Him do it. When He asks something, He gives the means to accomplish what He asks.

This virtue is so essential that she makes it one of the most characteristic of the spirituality proper to her Congregation.

*To be a true Sister of Notre Dame, one must possess the virtue of abandonment in its full extent:* abandoning oneself for life and for death, in consolations, and in dryness, in honor

[1] Cf. "Abandonment," *Dictionnaire de Spiritualité.*

and in dishonor. One must submit to all employments, to all assignments which Holy Obedience will make known; today here, tomorrow there, the whole earth is the Lord's; all must be the same to the Sisters of Notre Dame who have the happiness to follow after the apostles, according to the Spirit of our Holy Institute.

One will have noted those words: "All must be the same to the Sisters of Notre Dame." These words, in fact, recall those in the "Foundation" of the *Spiritual Exercises*. Saint Ignatius, on whom she had meditated and whom she understood so well, calls that abandonment, indifference, so as to bring out the universality of that abandonment and the detachment of heart which it requires. For this eminent Master of the spiritual life all spirituality must have for a foundation the conviction that all creatures, the most opposite on the surface, such as health and sickness, a long life and a short one, honor and dishonor, can in turn be the ways chosen by God, in His Providence, to sanctify us and to carry out His own plans. All are then equal in the eyes of God, provided we do the Will of God. Let us make use of everything at the present moment to praise Him, to reverence Him, and to serve Him. That only is good which His goodness gives and asks of us. On this point, as we might expect, Blessed Julie Billiart lived the essential doctrine of the "Foundation" of Saint Ignatius. And when her Religious meditate, they find in the writings of their Mother the smiling and attractive example of it, a sincere, real application of it.

Let us quote, to illustrate her thought yet more, that passage written by an eminent disciple of Saint Ignatius, which we might believe was written by Blessed Julie:

You must remember that God asks everything of you, and yet He asks nothing. He asks all because He wishes to reign over and in you as a possession which is His in every respect, in such a way that everything submits, everything obeys the least sign of His Will. He asks nothing of you because He wishes to do everything in you, without your having any part in it, but being content to be the subject on whom and in whom He acts, so that all the glory may be His, and that He alone may be known and praised eternally.

Thus spoke the Blessed Claude de la Colombiere.

From this "Foundation" of the *Spiritual Exercises,* it is logical that one acquire little by little serenity, simplicity, and childlikeness of heart.

Abandonment to Providence, when one practices it without reserve and with love, as did Blessed Julie, has *serenity* for an immediate effect. All the portraits of Blessed Julie which remain show her smiling, affable, as one who lacks nothing. The testimonies of those who dealt with her are unanimous. They are so numerous that one must send the reader to her biographer: "During the war, 1814–1815, they declare that firmness of soul of the Blessed Servant of God never failed. She lost neither her calmness, nor her sweet peace, although she had many cares concerning her convents located in the midst of the fighting. She encouraged her Sisters, not letting them yield to fear, but making them pray much."[1]

Blessed, a thousand times blessed are the souls who rely only on the good God. What a solid prop they have found. . . . Never will they be shaken. . . . A soul who puts all her trust

[1] Articles submitted for the Apostolic Process, p.33.

in God will enjoy deep tranquillity even in the midst of storms and tempests. . . . Do not indulge your imagination so much; your fears do not come from the good God.

They say that she was utterly firm in her resolutions. She made them under the guidance of the Holy Spirit. After her "election" nothing could make her change. "If . . . a project did not succeed, our Mother knew how to preserve intact the peace of her soul." The same serenity was noted in Saint Ignatius and in so many other Saints, but especially in all those who had a special devotion to Divine Providence.

Let us focus our attention on that point. We are not giving here a list of her many virtues, but we are trying to show the supernatural power of the faith which Blessed Julie had in the Goodness of God. For it is faith that primarily characterized her personal spirituality and that of her Daughters.

Fathers and theologians are not lacking who bring out the necessary and immutable bond between the virtues of serenity, peace, calmness, and intense joy with unreserved abandonment to Divine Providence. One would not understand the depth of the soul of Blessed Julie Billiart if one did not remember what Bossuet preached often with more emphasis than others:

Through Malachy He has said: "I am the Lord, and I do not change." God is absolutely perfect. Then "He who is perfect is happy": for he knows his perfection, since to know his perfection is too essential a part of perfection to be lacking in a perfect Being. O God, you are a happy God, I rejoice in your eternal happiness. . . .[1] Throughout Scripture we read that "the man who hopes is happy. . . ." So, too, Saint Paul speaks of You as *Happy.* "I tell you these things according to the glorious Gospel of the Blessed God" (I Tim. 1:11). And again: "This coming he in his own time will make manifest, who is the Blessed and only Sovereign, the King of Kings and Lord of Lords; who alone has immortality and dwells in light inaccessible, whom no man has seen nor can see, to whom be honor and everlasting dominion. Amen. Amen."[2]

From all this evidence, we must seek the source of the extraordinary serenity of Julie Billiart in her abandonment through love. She placed her happiness in the eternal felicity of God, which the innumerable manifestations of Providence do not change but reveal to men of great faith.

This constant serenity was sustained in all events, even the most varied, the most unforeseen, the most opposed to human equilibrium, in a life burdened with responsibilities and duties. It reigned equally over the complications of false or of mediocre virtue. That should be noted, because her spirituality is always characterized by *simplicity.*

What she wrote is original, in phraseology that seems elementary, but which reveals her profound views. Who has ever declared more than Saint Francis de Sales, that one reaches sanctity while trying to acquire simplicity?

Without simplicity there is no Sister of Notre Dame. This virtue must be the basis, the foundation of our holy Institute (Holy Rule, Art. 3).

[1] The Psalms make us repeat unceasingly that the man who hopes in God alone is happy: v.g. Ps. 64,83,88.93, 111,126,127,136, etc. Likewise frequently in Ecclesiasticus, Proverbs, etc.

[2] *Elevations sur les mysteres,* IIIe Elev.

I have told you, my dear Sisters, that those who are not simple are neither Daughters of the good God, nor mine.

My God, please give me good, simple Daughters, and I shall have treasures to fashion into good Sisters of Notre Dame.

Vocation is at stake here. If there are types of spirituality which do not lead souls to simplicity in their relations with God, with their Superiors, with their Sisters, with their neighbors in the apostolic life, Blessed Julie does not recognize them. She does not want such. This virtue so gripped her that one could compile a book with her writings concerning simplicity.

The analysis of simplicity made by Fenelon, it would seem, makes us see, through this great master of spiritual psychology, the depths of the thoughts of this great mystic soul. It should be useful to enlighten the religious of Notre Dame in their vocation.

Simplicity consists in seeing God only in all things. To arrive at perfect simplicity there are three degrees to compass: the first consists in suppressing the division in the soul that is interested at one and the same time in interior and exterior things.

The simple soul is conscious of its superiority over the things that attract and enchain it. It frees itself from the slavery of the senses, from the witchery of trifles, from the infatuation of the sensible. No more is it the plaything of events. No longer does it find itself scattered, divided, pulled about, but rather, unified by attention to the light which comes from within.

In the second degree another division disappears. In giving oneself to God one does not lose oneself. "He who wishes to save his life will lose it," said Our Lord (Mark 8:35).

One has not attained the simplicity of the second degree if, while loving God, one wishes to feel and to be assured that one does love Him, and if one wishes even to enjoy that love. Frequent self-examination produces in weak souls a kind of superstition which attaches to multiple trifles an almost sacred value, and in strong souls it produces a presumption which makes them esteem the activity of their nature more than that of God. The soul, busy with itself in its relations with creatures and with God, is full of itself, anxious about all that can disturb the complacency which it has in its own virtue. Trial revolts such a soul, because it sees the possibility of its complacency being disturbed. Fenelon said very shrewdly:

The soul who is in the world is inebriated with all that she sees *outwardly,* but this one, that is to say, the soul engrossed in self attains only the second degree of simplicity and is inebriated by all that she imagines she is doing within. But, in fact both are inebriated. Self-inebriation is worse than that concerned with exterior things, because it appears to be wisdom which it is not; one thinks little about curing it; one looks upon it as a glory, as an honor; one thinks of it as a power above honors and upon self as above the rest of men.

The simplicity which Blessed Julie Billiart had and which she required of her daughters is of the third degree; the first two are easier to understand.

In the third degree the soul forgets self; she sees herself only in God. She sees herself, to be sure, full of corruption, faults, and infidelities; but this knowledge does not turn from God by anxious reflections on her own worth. On the contrary by the light of God always present and good she sees herself face to face with His purity and His infinite paternity. This attention to the Love of God rouses in her the desire of the highest perfection possible, because all perfection, given or acquired, is the glory of the Father, His Will, His reign in her. God is her end; and if the glory and the Will of God are not evident in her as a first end, her states become "indifferent" although painful.

Blessed Julie requires this simplicity first of all in *relations with God*. She describes it perfectly as a soul which has experienced it. She shuns what we have called the first degree of simplicity, study, reasonings, refinement of soul. But she humbles herself, adores, listens, and speaks familiarly with God, as a child "who knows that her Father loves her, and that this Father is infinitely good and omnipotent," as a Spouse "who makes use of her rights over the heart of a Spouse who can and who wishes to please her."

She requires simplicity *in relations with Superiors*. The complex soul "is defiant, examines, murmurs sometimes," and while it carries out orders mechanically "in the depths of its heart, it resists." All retrospection disappears in a simple soul "who does all that is commanded without questioning." "A complex soul will never make a good Sister of Notre Dame," said Blessed Julie.

### SIMPLICITY IN RELATIONS WITH THE SISTERS

The complex soul regulates its conduct on personal merits, not on compatability of characters; the simple soul knows that "whatever is of value in the creature comes from the immutable Being, from Infinite Perfection." Then her admiration soars to God to Whom alone she attributes all her glory.

## SIMPLICITY IN THE VICISSITUDES OF LIFE

We must not omit here the admirable analysis which she makes of a simple soul:

A simple soul is always content, in times of dryness as in times of consolation, because her great submission to the holy and adorable Will of God makes her accept with love and gratitude all that her good Father in Heaven sends her; she loves, adores, and kisses the Hand that strikes her. Having offered herself to God she is happy that He deigns to accept her oblation. When a soul is firmly rooted in the virtue of simplicity, nothing can move her, neither the changes of place nor of time, neither afflictions, nor embarrassment; nothing surprises her, nothing disturbs her, because she knows that it is God who does and who permits everything, and because she loves the good God so much she would not know how not to smile at His good pleasure in her regard, whatever it be. Sometimes, it is true, she feels great repugnances, but she surmounts them by despising them, by distracting her attention, going ahead always, pretending not to see them.

Among the impressive writings of the Saint of Lisieux, we admit humbly that we have found nothing which surpasses these excerpts from Blessed Julie. We wish sincerely that many religious orders would preserve in their Institutes treasures as precious from their Founders.

In the *Apostolate,* she recommended that this simplicity be guarded. But this is a topic to which we must return later.

The last characteristic which we admire as essential to abandonment and to the paternal Providence of God is *joy of heart*.

What does this expression mean? A childlike spirit, in which sadness has no place or is evaporated immediately by a warm heart.

The soul given to abandonment remains always as carefree as a child, or it is not perfectly abandoned. It treats as familiarly with God as He acted with His Mother Mary in the crib and at Nazareth. All pictures which represent Jesus with the Holy Virgin when He was three or four years old have emphasized the divine tenderness of the Child and His Mother; the simple soul should imitate Jesus and His Mother. Respect, liberty, straightforwardness, spontaneity, openness, candor—these and other similar words which intimate filial respect express what we call childlikeness of heart with God. And when the good God, the good Heavenly Father, tries the soul, such a soul seeks refuge in His arms, as the Child Jesus would throw Himself, with all His childish strength, on the Heart of Mary during their long journey in exile.

But youthfulness of heart should flourish always in the community and in all relations with the neighbor.

The soul is all to all, joyous with those who are gay, to increase their joy; sad with those in sorrow, to console them. Always smiling, open, forgetful of self, she welcomes all who approach her, lends herself to all their desires; like a plaything in the hands of another she gives herself up as a common toy which each one may use as she pleases, not calling attention to it if some one has abused her, snubbed her, or wounded her. As the light is always fresh and for the common use, so victims are "consumed" by all. She does not complain of being at the mercy of others; she gives herself up for their convenience, no matter the hour. At the same time she does not compromise without grave reasons. She takes for granted the love of all, the sincerity of all, the simplicity of all, superiors or inferiors. And her attitude is so gracious that others deal with her, without calculating, without reticence: simple, confiding, affectionate. Nothing is more contagious than youthfulness of heart. She can be very daring; naïve, hazardous attempts are natural to her; she takes risks with others with an ease that forces hearts to respond to her, above all cold hearts that seek for warmth, gloomy hearts which seek sunshine, closed-up hearts that seek a smile. Near her one lives, so to speak, on the Riviera.

Youthfulness of heart has more attractiveness and more power than all the talents which vaunt their superiority and their moral authority. The influence that it exercises is as that of a child, gentle, secret, silent, indirect, penetrating. One accepts it without precaution, because it does not wound sensibility, vanity; it does not touch some hidden awkwardly. One defends oneself when it is necessary to counter the prestige of a man who imposes on personal liberty, but one submits without hesitation to the delicate strength of a child as to the perfume of a violet, because it acts unconsciously.

By these characteristics we describe the spiritual character of Blessed Julie. Let us not think that smiling joyousness of spirit is a superficial virtue. On the contrary we touch on an intimate secret of the Presence of the good God in a soul given to abandonment. As the Psalm recommends: "Be glad in the Lord and rejoice . . . that I may exalt in thy love" (Ps. 31). God effects in me pleasure, delight, charm. He permits me to love, to find pleasure; He wills that everything shall redound to my good. Saint Augustine has often spoken of that effect of the Goodness of God. "Free will," he says, "is capable only of sin, if the way of truth is hidden from it, and when it begins to see the truth, there is no pleasure in it."[1] And again: "Where the Spirit is, there is no pleasure in sinning, and that is liberty. Where the Spirit is not, sin is pleasure, and that is slavery."[2]

And again: "One does not wish to do what is just or good either because one does not know that it is just or good, or because knowing it, one does not like it. . . . What makes one see that of which one is ignorant? What makes that pleasant which is not pleasing? Grace."[3]

Did Saint Augustine discover in his time the intimate secret of the abiding youthfulness that later characterized Mere Julie? Her life and her personal writings are completely colored by the reflection of joy which comes from the radiance of the Goodness of God.

Perhaps Mere Julie would use different words to express the state of her soul, rather than the expression: youthfulness of soul. Words, however, must needs vary in order to convey something so close to the Nature of God. The terms of peace and serenity recur most often. She experiences "the richness" of this peace, as says the Scripture, more than one can say. It has been compared to the sea when it comes in full tide to the earth, when the waters are naturally calm, when there is not a trace of wind. Then it comes in majesty

---

[1] *De Spiritu et Littera*, III,5;P.L.:XLIV,203.
[2] *Idem.* XLIV,218.
[3] *Idem*, XLIV,167.

and magnificence. So divine peace brings an effusion from God "Who is so good." With it come the gifts of God and the riches of His Kingdom.

Such was the soul of Blessed Julie. She would gulp down into her abyss of peace all that flowed into its pure waters and which might make her suffer.

To achieve the marvellous effects which her inviolable faith in the goodness of God produced in the soul of the Foundress we must make evident a leading intention which reminds one of Saint Ignatius. She wished only one thing: the Will of God, or to phrase it in more general language, the *Glory of God*.

The Glory of God results from the manifestation to men of His transcendent, incomparable, unique Being; then from His love, and likewise from His goodness.

God is glorified when men recognize His goodness and when they respond to it with generous liberality.

To understand properly the thought of the Blessed Foundress one must compare it to what Saint Ignatius says on this point, and not minimize it while comparing it with the sublime purpose of this great apostle. For her whole life is witness that she sought only the glory of God. This is, in truth, the purpose of the virtues and of the good works of all religious orders. But, like the Founder of the Company of Jesus, she aimed at *the Greater Glory of God*.

An article in the review *Christus* has cited numerous texts from Scripture, from Saint Ignatius, and from his first companions, which establish the fact that the Company was founded to procure the greatest possible glory to God. Some details will make clearer the words and intentions of Blessed Julie.

A triple consequence results for her as for Saint Ignatius from this magnanimous choice of the greater glory of God.

To begin with, this glory, which, as we have said, consists in the most extensive adoration and love possible among the creatures, should be the supreme end of all works that each, according to his measure of grace from the Holy Spirit, during his earthly life and eternally may reflect the majesty and the mercy of God. Without doubt this is necessarily the end of all virtues and of all Christian apostolates. But each religious order attains this end by particular means organized around a central idea, as teaching, the care of the sick, social service work, the liturgy, hospitality.

But Saint Ignatius wished before any project, and not as a consequence of a project, to propose to souls the glory of God in its universality. In this way one is not content to offer to God what one does, but one intends to do what one believes will give more glory to God, adored and loved above all. Hence in the phrase, "To the Greater Glory of God," the emphatic word is the least apparent: "greater." That is why in His Company and in the *Spiritual Exercises* the little adverb "more" recurs constantly, to show that it will not suffice to be virtuous but that virtue must surpass itself always, with the grace of God. Did not Jesus Christ glorify His Father by means so extraordinary that God only could have imagined greater?

Saint Ignatius wished that the glory of God be sought for itself, with such purity of intention that every consideration of personal advantage, as well in the acquiring of virtues as in the development of human perfections be, as it were, removed from the mind. God alone should have first place.

Forgetfulness of self and forgetfulness of all else should be total, lest God be sought only partially, secondarily, and under certain conditions. God is transcendent over the creature, as He is infinitely supreme Himself. The nakedness of the Crucified between two thieves and His ignominious death are two secondary things which should not be rejected if God is more glorified by this means rather than by others, more human.

Finally, the greater glory of God is not measured by human intelligence and capacities. God alone makes it known by His Providence, by the Church, by the inspiration of the Holy Spirit, by authority. Any resistance to the "known Will of God," to the interior inspiration of the Holy Spirit, to obedience, can be justified by no reason, by no vain pretext. For the greater glory of God is always the work of grace that gives the powers which we can have only if God grants them to us. God is at once He who proposes perfection and He who supplements our powerlessness. One sees, then, the consequences of that maxim. Anything against the good pleasure of God, whatever it may be, and however ambitious and surprising it may appear, the soul can never offer as a pretext for her weakness, her objections, her indignities, because she has the assurance that the glory of God belongs to God and is His work alone.

In imitation of Saint Ignatius, Blessed Julie Billiart proposed this ideal in its most sparkling purity, and her life shows that she never tried to evade the most exacting desires of God under any pretext. She advised the same per-

fection to her Daughters. It suffices to read her admirable
letters to be persuaded that she always united to a most
tender gentleness the express will to tend, with the help of
grace, to the highest sanctity, and to the most perfect
actions.[1]

Let us summarize briefly—while regretting the brevity—
the analysis which reveals the grandeur and the beauty of
that soul, like a crypt in a cathedral, in its magnificent
spirituality. For there are so many things to include in
speaking of the preferred object of her love: "The Heart
of the Incarnate Son of God."

The cry of this soul, "Ah! How good He is, the good
God," could have been—if we had not sought the spiritual
richness of it—only a simple ejaculatory prayer, such as are
spoken by the thousand by pious souls. It is the expression
of a soul filially devoted to the Heavenly Father, who is
always near, the filial spirit of Jesus in the Gospel. Jesus
consummated the fullness of His sanctity in this filial spirit,
and one sees clearly that all His virtues of an infinite value
are, so to speak, the multiple echoes of one principal note:
the love of the Son for the Father. What one calls abandonment, confidence, union of will, obedience, serenity,
purity of intention, fidelity, courage, sublime and tender
outbursts of His prayer, all the magnanimities of His actions and of His sufferings in reparation for sins—all, all in

[1] It is interesting to note that from the time of the Co-Foundress the
*Manual of Prayers* in use by the Sisters of Notre Dame (1831) bore
the device: "To the Greater Glory of God." It may be seen under the
image of the Immaculate Conception. In the first article of the Rule we
read: "The end of the Congregation is to procure the greater glory of
God."

Him is adoration of the Father, love of the Father, glory to the Father.

This is how one must understand the cry of Blessed Julie: "Ah! He is good, the good God!"

The first part of our analysis will have proved this, we hope, especially to the readers of her life and of her writings.

It may seem, then, that devotion to Jesus Christ and especially to the Sacred Heart may not be necessary to attain to sanctity.

This supposition is contrary to faith, since we must believe one comes to the Father only through Jesus Christ; it is contrary also to the spirituality of Blessed Julie Billiart, for if one deprives her of union with her Spouse, Jesus, one despoils her of one of the greatest splendors of her holiness.

*Who shall separate us from the
Love of Christ?* (ROM. 8:35)

# 2 Spouse of the Son of God

If one wants to explore the spirituality of
Blessed Julie Billiart in all its dimensions, one
must necessarily enter closely into her relationship with Jesus, the Son of God. For it is by the
Son of God that the Christian can reach the
Father—and it is in the Son of God that he becomes a child of the Father. "No one comes to
the Father but through Me" (John 14:6).

Saints are not made by theology, nor by exege-
sis, nor by history. It is not science that has led
them to sanctity, but it is the infinitely holy life
of Christ in them. In proportion as they are of
Christ, in Christ, members of Christ, they have
been saints; for there is no other sanctity in

humanity than that of Christ, spread out over all those whom the Father has called. Mystics, endowed with most extraordinary gifts, cannot claim any other privilege than that of belonging wholly to Christ.

Saint John of the Cross speaks thus on this subject[1]:

If you study Him well you will find all in Him, because He is My whole discourse, My reply, all My vision and revelation, Whom I have already spoken of, expanded, demonstrated, and revealed, giving Him to you for brother, for companion, for master, for prize, and for recompense. . . . I descended upon Him with My Spirit on Mount Thabor, saying: "This is My well beloved Son in Whom I am well pleased. Hear ye Him. . . ." If you want Me to console you, look at My Son who is so submissive and obedient to Me for love of Me, He who is afflicted, and you will hear what He will reply to you. If you want Me to tell you hidden things or events, cast your eyes on Him and you will find hidden mysteries and the Wisdom and the wonders of God which are within Him, according to the word of the Apostle: "In Whom, the Son of God, are hidden all the treasures of wisdom and of knowledge." Some treasures of wisdom will be more sublime for you, more savoury, more useful than you want to know now. For that the same Apostle was glorified, saying that it had been given to him to understand "that he knew only Jesus Christ and Jesus crucified." And if you want other visions, and divine or corporal revelations, look upon Him in His humanity and there you will find more than you expect, because the Apostle says also that "all the fullness of the Divinity dwells in Christ corporally."

Between Christ and us virtues do not differ, for ours are the reflections of His virtues, manifestations in sinful flesh of His holiness; all our rights, all our titles, all our worth come from His, and from no other source. There is only one difference between what glorifies Him and what glorifies us: it is in the

[1] *Ascent of Mount Carmel*, 1,II,22.

unique manner in which He depends on the Father. His union with the Father is the same as that of the Trinity, where the Three Persons are one God, whilst ours is gratuitous, accidental, pure favor, an outflow of mercy. "My Father and I are one." "All that is thine is Mine, and all that is Mine is thine."

This is a fundamental truth to hold in all solid spirituality and especially in that of our Blessed Julie where it is very evident. That is why we insist on it. The indwelling of Christ in us and of us in Christ, the indwelling of the Father in Christ and of Christ in the Father, are two mysteries closely allied to each other, and Jesus reveals this to us several times in the Gospels. "Eternal life is to know Thee, the only true God, and Jesus Christ whom Thou hast sent." This knowledge makes us like to God. "We know that when he appears, we shall be like to him, for we shall see him just as he is" (I John 3:2). "In that day you will know that I am in the Father, and you in Me, and I in you" (John 14:20). It will then become reciprocal indwelling completely realized, today begun by theological virtues, as Jesus had asked in His supreme prayer: "That all may be one, even as thou, Father, in me and I in thee; that they may be one in us (John 17:21). "That they may be one as we are, I in them and you in me, that they may be perfected in unity" (John 17:22–23). "And I have made known to them thy name, and will make it known, in order that the love with which thou hast loved me may be in them, and I in them" (John 17:26).

In all these texts and others as well, the supreme unity of the Father and of the Son appear as *the ideal model and as the fruitful source, as the effectual origin of the unity of Christians with Christ and with one another*. The bond of this unity is love, love born of the knowledge of God. Love seeks to accomplish His Will; then God reveals Himself more and more.

Those eyes which are opened, that faith which is enlightened, and which contemplates God and Christ, that Love which stretches out to the Supreme Good and gives herself to Him without reserve, is a new life which transforms the soul into Jesus Christ. Knowledge blossoms out in it necessarily. "You will see me because I live and you, too, will live." God is not the God of the dead but of the living.[1]

There we have some reminders from the Gospel which explain the theological foundation of the relations of faith and of love which Julie Billiart had with Jesus Christ, and consequently, all her eminent virtues. We must insist on the Passion of Jesus, for which her soul had an intense devotion. But let us consider first how deeply she loved Jesus Christ with the love of a spouse.

Her virtuous life is the life of a spouse, and her life of a spouse is a life of union with Him who has sought to be "the Spouse of souls." She is not wise, pious, obedient, chaste, poor, faithful to all the desires of God as Jesus was before her and for her the example of these virtues; but she is wise, pious, obedient, and perfect in all things in Jesus, because Jesus within her is thus, because if He were not so, life in Him would no longer be that of a spouse, but the wretched life of any other woman. It is of prime importance not to call that true virtue, which is only the likeness of the virtue of Jesus, and not His own holy life as Son of the Father in all the adopted Sons of the Father.

The Spirit effects this marvellous unity as no other crea-

[1] Lebreton, S.J., *Tu solus sanctus*, p. 29.

ture can do; it is the effect of faith and of love which the
Spirit of Jesus diffuses in our hearts.

It is a truth, illustrated today and focused in all its fullness by theologians of the day, but forcefully admitted by
Saint Paul, by the Fathers, especially by Saint Augustine,
that all our supernaturally good actions are actions of particular members of a Mystical Body, that of Jesus.

Blessed Julie was specially enlightened in this doctrine
which directed her religious life. More than a hundred
times, perhaps, eager for the most profound union with
Jesus—even to the point of identification, it was remarked
sometimes—she repeated words like the following, or even
more zealous:

Oh! yes, all my dear good Daughters, I place all my wishes
for you in the Heart of our good Jesus: that you may all become the servants of the Lord, to whom we are all consecrated,
our body, our soul, our mind. *Everything* in our conduct should
be *Jesus*. Oh! my good Daughters, how sweet it is to live by
dying every moment to our own life, to live so that the spirit
of our lovable Jesus only may live in us! (Reply to New Year
wishes, 1807.)

The life of our loving Jesus requires that we should become
very like to Him: gentle, patient, charitable, supporting one
another. Oh! the beautiful life of our good Jesus in our hearts!
He wishes to live alone in the hearts of my dear Daughters.
Live Jesus!

She kept repeating this theme: "May we become other
Jesus Christs." The prayer *Anima Christi* summarizes her
thoughts, because therein the soul asks that all in it be
transformed into Jesus Christ. As we do not wish to over-
emphasize testimonies to her devotion, we shall limit our-

selves to two points which shine forth with exceptional brilliance in her life: *her love of Jesus Crucified on the Cross and in the Blessed Sacrament,* and *her love of the Heart of Christ,* pierced and gaping open for us on the Cross.

These two references of her soul are due to her consecration as a spouse; she wished to be "only one" with Jesus Christ, through love. Then, inasmuch as she would not be "one" on the Cross with her Spouse, and in His immolated Body, and in His Blood shed in the Sacrament, she was certain to be united only partially and superficially. That would have been a resistance, an infidelity to grace, to be content to serve Him in the joy of fidelity.

The desire of Jesus to mark her with the seal of His Wounds was evident in her early life, for her family, tried by the reverses of fortune and by sickness, could not give her the joys of childhood, but only the happiness which little Julie experienced in her devotedness.

At the end of the year of 1764, when she was scarcely twelve years old, she lost her sister Marie Louise, and shortly after, her brother, Jean Baptiste. One of her younger sisters was almost blind; her little brother was lame. One can sense, under these conditions, the thousand privations of her existence. Little Julie, alone with her mother, took charge of the cares of the household. Those who have been well off or have known the happiness of home life where one's wishes were always gratified do not know what daily privation of the most necessary things is for a child and for a young girl. For such a one sensibility and imagination are dried up as flowers without water. The adult struggles against poverty and hopes to triumph over it. The child endures and hopes for nothing.

The poverty of a family in a home where there are children is often a stimulant to desires to appear well to do. But little Julie had no desire to be freed from her cross, as from a prison. God made her love, cherish, and admire her cross as a pearl of great price. For He wanted her crucified as Jesus. By a very strange intervention of Providence (a stone thrown, a gun fired, a criminal attempt on the life of her father), she entered into a dolorous union with Christ crucified. In 1774, suddenly, a malady tortured her poor weakened body. She was then twenty-three years old. In 1782 the good God intervened again, to make her share in a new scene of the Passion of Jesus. The surgeon of the village thought to cure her by many blood-lettings, and the state of the young girl was aggravated by this treatment; thus she was, as it were, fixed to a gibbet, nailed as if by four nails, during twenty-two years. All that time she did not leave her bed or a chair by which they wheeled her around sometimes. History tells that, unable to move, she suffered from "nervous contractions, from almost continual insomnia, from violent crises which seemed to bring her to an agony. Five times she received Extreme Unction." She was in utter anguish seeing the burden she had become for her parents.

Who could have imagined that God was preparing her to be the Foundress of a great religious apostolic congregation?

God had in mind, less a new creation for the service of the Church, than a true and deep spirituality. For it is impossible that the thought of adult age should not be the development of the trends of youth. We say *true spirituality,* because all spirituality which is not rooted in Calvary and whose sap is not the Blood of Christ, arises from a religion foreign to Christianity. We say *deep spirituality* also. For there is nothing deeper than the love of God manifested by the pierced Heart of Jesus Christ and by His glorious Wounds. All the rest in the religious life, according to God, is accessory and superficial.

Reverend Mother Saint Joseph, co-foundress, heard Mere Julie say that she had never experienced the least ennui on her cross, as she was united to her Saviour; and what strengthened this union was the "cruel abandonment" to which she was subjected by the privation of the sacraments when Cuvilly was governed by a schismatic pastor. During the three hours of His Crucifixion Our Lord was consoled only by the words of the Good Thief, by the mute presence of His helpless Mother, by the tears of the disciple whom He loved, and by some lonely women. In view of her future He acted differently to His servant. Paralyzed by sorrow, He gave her the interior joy of teaching the catechism to some children and of converting all sorts of people, who were attracted by the superhuman beauty of her soul.

When one ignores the design of Providence, one may imagine that Our Lord tried Julie only once, to form her. Let us not be so deceived. There are depths in the souls of the saints where suffering can always penetrate. Julie Billiart, in keeping with the divine way, was tested in her union even with Jesus on the Cross. For the revolution attacked her through the priests who had taken the oath. These persecuted the faith and the charity of this holy one who talked too much of them, and who opposed them forcefully with Catholic truth, the holiness of the Church, the devotion to the Passion and to the Blessed Sacrament.

What irritated the "patriots" more was the fact that she concealed good priests. They chased her out, they pursued her, they trailed her from village to village at the cost of unimaginable sufferings. They prepared to burn her alive on a pile of faggots formed of a cross, tabernacles, statues of Saints, and by other relics of pillaged churches. She was sheltered at Compiegne, where she found a little room and an excellent priest, M. Lamarche, who praised her virtues highly.

There it was that Jesus, in His providential design, spoke to her for the first time. "Julie," said Pere Clare in his biography, "was rapt in ecstasy and saw rising up before the eyes of her soul the mountain of Calvary. Grouped around Jesus on His Cross she saw a multitude of virgins wearing a religious garb unfamiliar to her. The vision was so clear, the faces of some of the religious so clearly etched on her memory, that many years afterwards she could say to some of those who made application to enter the Congregation: "God wishes you in our Society; I saw you at Compiegne . . ." Towards the close of that vision Julie heard these words, referring to those who had been shown to her: *"They are the Daughters whom I give you in the Institute which will be marked by My Cross."*

This vision recalls that of Saint Ignatius, in the chapel of Storta, where the Founder of the Company of Jesus saw the Father with Jesus carrying His Cross.

Those are two visions which are of equal importance in characterizing the Company of Jesus and that of the Sisters of Notre Dame; they reveal in advance the Will of God for both religious congregations, which resemble each other as brother and sister.

In continual suffering for twenty-two years, Julie thought only of thanking God for granting her the great gift of sharing His Passion.

Thus, when she arrived at Amiens, a journey which had been a veritable torture, she wrote:

I pass whole days, thanks be to God (Let no one omit that parenthetical phrase!) suffering much, and nights which are sometimes worse. But, my good tender Friend, what is it that I suffer in comparison with all that our Lord willed to suffer for love of me! When the good God gives me grace to suffer more, I shall offer some of my suffering for all my good friends in the faith.

In a miraculous manner, through obedience, she was almost completely cured of physical suffering at the age of fifty-three years. Pere Enfantin, in fact, had ordered her to walk in order to show her faith in the love and in the power of the Heart of Jesus. She obeyed; she walked.

The Passion of Christ, according to the common teaching of the Church, was not partial. Christ suffered not only in His body, but also in His heart, in His intelligence, and in His soul.

All the Saints have not been called, as was Blessed Julie, to feel the sufferings of Christ in their totality. Jesus alone knew the depth of the abyss of each of her sufferings, but He gives the grace to certain Saints to taste at once their bitterness and to experience the union of their being annihilated with that of Jesus.

That was a favor granted to the Foundress of the Sisters of Notre Dame. Chapter titles in the official biography of Julie give evidence of this: Contradictions (X), Painful Struggles (XI), Expulsion (XII), Emigration (XIII), Rehabilitation (VI), War and Invasion (XVIII), Last Crosses (XIX).

In those many pages there is a summary of tortures which one would call martyrdom if the body and not the soul were the victim of them.

Our purpose is to show the greatness of the sanctity of Mere Julie, when she lacked everything *"except the good God."* Faith shines out, then, no doubt, in all its purity and inflames charity.

In July, 1793, she saw the heroic Carmelites mount the scaffold. She thought of only one thing: What happiness it would be for her to give up her life for Jesus Christ. In September, 1795, when she lost her aged mother, she wrote thus: "You understand what my sensitive heart experiences now, although it is completely submissive, by the grace of God, to the decrees of Providence."

Let us read attentively the following sentences: "It is always by the path of sacrifices that He leads me to Him, to Him alone. Ask, then, for me that I may be immolated to the good pleasure of the Divine Master."

When Pere Varin, at the beginning of the nineteenth century told her that she was called by the Most High to dedicate herself to the education of youth, Julie was at that time completely paralyzed and her sufferings were very acute. Pere Varin, nevertheless, ordered her in the name of God to get to work at once. Providence compelled her and forbade her at the same time from undertaking that work which, in her condition, seemed to her so foolish. One must have experienced contradictions in one's conscience to know the price one must pay for peace. But she had found a conquering force in a thought which she repeated frequently in her prayers: "Lord, if you do not want me to serve You, to win souls, give me back my infirmities."

But from the day on which God asked her to found a Religious Congregation and schools, she practiced virtue—or to speak more exactly—all virtues, in an extraordinary manner. For her sufferings of mind, heart, and soul, exceeded all measure; those of her body were aggravated while she spiritualized them. According to the *Memoirs* of Mere Blin de Bourdon, one day Julie made this expressive speech to her: "I must yet undergo persecution." I replied to her as the Apostle Peter did to our Lord: "No, Ma Mere, this shall not be to you; you suffered all at Amiens." "I was told," she replied, "that I would be persecuted by bishops, priests and by the Sisters: and so all is not over." Pere Enfantin had spoken that truth in advance, without imagining that persecution were possible.

In order to understand how bishops, priests, and Sisters of Notre Dame could plot against her whose sanctity they recognized; how the devil could be served by consecrated persons in order to be grossly uncharitable and unjust towards her, calumniating her, attributing false statements and evil intentions to her, robbing her unjustly under cover of legality, but as thieves, of that which was needful for the support of her Community and of poor children, we must remember that He who was accused of being a seducer, ungodly, a blasphemer, unfaithful to the Law, a despiser of the Sabbath, an enemy of the religion of Israel, etc., was Jesus, the Son of God. Did they not treat her as a fool, as Jesus was treated at the palace of Herod? But the saints do not wear the white robe of injustice and of humiliation as do other men. Mere Julie Billiart, looking at Jesus only, was silent. Her spirituality was deeply rooted in the mystery of the Passion. She recognized the faults, the meannesses of her persecutors and excused them with respect, because of their priesthood, although the truth was on her side. Of what good would it be to air here "the wrongs which M. de Sambucy and the Bishop of Amiens were guilty of in the case of Julie?" It is sufficient to recall what M. Lamarche said, and he knew Mere Julie so well:

It would be sufficient to speak to her, to see her, to be convinced that the Spirit of God ruled her thoughts, her sentiments, her whole conduct. God permitted that she pass through great trials, that she be thwarted in all her projects. She groaned under so many interferences. But never did she lose her peace, nor the tranquillity of her soul. Always watchful over herself, she spoke to her ecclesiastical Superiors only with respect.

When, expelled from Amiens and without carrying anything with them, the Sisters arrived at Namur, they "had been deprived of every temporal resource; all the more and above all did they rely on Divine Providence." But they had been turned out only after very humiliating condemnations. Who could have believed it of a priest so esteemed as Pere Varin? Too credulous, he had listened to the tongues of calumny, which Saint James stigmatizes so violently, and had abandoned the poor Mother Julie to her fate, while passing severe judgment on her. In reply the holy

Mother had written to her confidante, Mere Blin de Bourdon:

> Man proposes and God disposes. Always, in every event, may His most just and most holy Will be done. . . . The good God wishes souls to have great confidence in Him, yes, a very great confidence. Live our good Jesus! Live His Holy Cross! . . . Let us love it, let us carry it. May it be our whole happiness. . . .

Let us say at once that Pere Varin was not obstinate in his error; he was completely convinced of the sanctity of his spiritual daughter. After her death, he summed up in one characteristic his appreciation of her life, when he declared that he had known in that exceptional soul "one who on earth lived only by love."

It is difficult to understand the pretexts which some enlightened individuals put forward against her; by their office and by grace they were in general benevolent people. An ecclesiastic of high degree, bishops, religious treated her as a "criminal" or as a schemer or a fool, when her virtues testified superlatively of the presence of Jesus in her. But Satan had had the cleverness, which is successful always, to form a "party" under the direction of an influential ecclesiastic, M. de Sambucy.[1]

Nothing is blinder than a party; and when it is hostile, it is blind to everything; it finds nothing good in an enemy whom it wants to crush. Let us admire Mere Julie, the soul who in the midst of an outburst of injuries and of calumnies, showed "no more resentment than a newly born

---

[1] Although Pere Varin was a religious of high competence, he let himself be drawn into this party. Pledged by the party, he said that Mere Julie and Mere Blin were two fools, and that M. de Sambucy should revise the rules which the Mothers had drawn up at Amiens.

infant," as Mere Blin de Bourdon testified concerning Mere
Julie.

Even more, she never weakened in her love of the Cross.
She wrote:

Let us look well with the eyes of faith, at our actual trials.
The Cross is the most excellent gift that God can give to His
children. I have seen somewhere that the more the good God
prepares a cross for a soul, the more light and graces He prepares for that soul. So, let us try to help one another to carry
the crosses which He destines for us.

One must have been expelled from one's home and from
one's country, to understand that the word *expulsion* is like
the word *fire*: a multitude of sufferings is enclosed in this
destruction of a past, so long and so painfully built up.

In Belgium the benevolence of the Bishops could not be
called a reparation, but only an encouragement.

At Namur, in spite of the protection of the Bishops,
things did not go much better than in the Diocese of
Amiens. The *Memoirs* of Mere Blin remark justly "the
frightful anger of Satan against the Congregation was to
blame." The Sisters, crushed by work, inexperienced, were
a prey to a contagious discouragement, which deprived
them of all strength and confidence. Once more, here we
refer to the sanctity of the Mother Foundress as a rock
where the foundations of a tower have been dug. She wrote
thus to Sister Eulalie:

My dear Child, it must needs be that our Institute be built
on the foundation of the Cross. Oh yes, all institutions destined
to procure the glory of God have great crosses. Let us accept
the trials which come to us from the Hand of our good Father.

Let us rest calmly in His holy Will, submitting ourselves for His Love in all sorts of privations.

All these heartaches, those of soul as well as those that are mental, since they come from ecclesiastical authorities, must have an end. The Psalms reiterate to the afflicted soul that God never leaves one alone in affliction.

According to the multitude of my sorrows in my heart, thy comforts have given joy to my soul (Ps. 93:19).
But the Lord is my refuge: and my God the help of my hope.
And He will render them their iniquity: and in their malice he will destroy them: the Lord our God will destroy them (Ps. 93:22–23).

Her letters have the same accent of confidence as the Psalms. Who does not find in this letter and in others like it the echo of the words of the Psalmist:

It is the good God who has taken our cause in hand. Oh! yes, my good tender Friend, the good God would have sent us an Angel from Heaven rather than let us fall into illusion, since we were so intent on accomplishing His Holy Will. Mindful of how faithful the good God is in His promises, we put all our trust in Him.

In this confidence, she entered upon the vocation to which God had called her:

Can one believe that the good God would abandon those who have had to leave their dear solitude to come to help poor little souls, souls plunged into the most profound darkness, deprived of the knowledge of our Lord Jesus Christ?

A new light was shed on her vocation by Monseigneur de Broglie, Bishop of Ghent. As a messenger of God he showed her, without perhaps seeing the full import of his words, that she was to do good not only in the limits of one diocese or a few dioceses, but, as was the case of Saint Ignatius and his Company, she was called to proclaim the glory of God in the whole Church. "You are not to remain in one Diocese. No, Mere Julie, your vocation is to go throughout the world."

Such was the reward, perhaps the greatest reward of her obedience, often crucifying, to the Bishops of France and of Belgium, this call from God, like that which Jesus addressed to His Apostles: "You will receive strength, the strength of the Holy Spirit who will descend upon you. Then you will be my witnesses in Jerusalem and in all Judea and Samaria and to the utmost bounds of the earth."

We shall see that this message of Monsignor de Broglie was prophetic. From the beginning of the century there had been founded in Belgium, besides the house at Namur (1807), those of Jumet (1808), Ghent (1809), Saint Hubert (1809), Zele (1811), Gembloux (1813), Fleurus and Andemne (1814), Liege and Dinant (1816), Thuin (1817). Before her death the Foundress had opened at least ten houses. We shall tell of the extraordinary blessings which, as the wind carries the seed afar, carried the Daughters of Mere Julie quickly over many countries of the world, to make flourish the spirit we have shown to be characteristic of their Institute.

But before concluding the pages showing her devotion to the Passion of Christ, we should tell of the last crosses

of her admirable life, for until her very death she was crucified, like Jesus.

One can imagine what an anxiety to the Mother of a
religious Congregation was the invasion of a country by
soldiers in war, undisciplined, given up to their evil inclinations, and excited by the irritation of confusion. After
the Battle of Leipzig, when Napoleon lost a great battle,
the remnants of his great Army were thrown into Belgium,
wounded, ragged, worn out. That was an opportunity for
the Sisters of Notre Dame de Namur to devote themselves
with heroic charity and, perhaps, foolishness, to the care of
those with contagious diseases, starving, wounded, dying.
Russians and Prussians entered Namur. The cost of the
most ordinary living increased in enormous proportions. We
are not so far from invasions by victorious armies not to
know by experience the tragic consequences of these
famines. Mere Julie wrote in anguish: "Ours is a very
unhappy city; for we must provide all the troops with
brandy, bread, and meat." But the threats of hunger, sickness, and death were nothing compared with the diabolical
terrors of the women and Religious because of the unre-
strained violence of these brutal men. We are not dreaming
it. In her *Memoirs,* Mere Blin de Bourdon wrote of the
terrors which reigned in their houses, besieged by intoxicated and lawless troops. She trusted Providence with a
confidence that perhaps only she could have. She barricaded
the doors and exterior gates of the house, however. "The
soldiers," the *Memoirs* say, "came many times, day and
night, knocking loudly at the door with all their might. We
avoided the least noise, we kept out of sight; no bells were
rung." History also takes care to say that "Mere Julie was

everywhere: during the day she guarded the doors . . . at night, she prayed in the chapel, where she heard the blows on the doors, struck by soldiers and marauders."

A letter written by Mere Julie reveals her virtue. She entrusted all her religious family, including the children in the schools, to the Holy Virgin and to our Lord.

If the good God is for us, who shall be against us? They wanted to frighten us at Namur, as they have done everywhere; but we have put all our confidence in the Lord. We are very calm. We pray as much as we can. . . . We must see all in God. Let us love Him, my Daughter, and let us place all our cares in His amiable Providence.

Only Saints write such beautiful things.

During all this time of ruins and of plunderings which one can scarcely imagine, but which we tell not just for the pleasure of dramatizing the history of the Congregation, the Foundress found time "to write numerous letters to her Daughters, to keep up their courage."

One is impressed by the tenderness, the gaiety of soul, the firmness of courage which are evident in the pages of her correspondence at this time. Nay more, one finds therein, like white flowers and red flowers, the candor, the simplicity, the modesty of the insatiable love of the Cross, and of confidence in God, carried to the point of heroism.

Everything passes. War, like a thunderstorm, when it has finished pillaging the beauty of a country, carries its destructive powers to other regions.

But war is a scourge; misunderstanding in a city, or in a family, and with still stronger reason in a religious family, is another scourge. A soul as holy and as delicate as that of

Mere Julie Billiart, must be more sensitive to this kind of torture than to war itself, where the enemy attacks from within and in spite of humility, tests the bonds of affection and of unity of spirit.

Before her death Julie experienced these last crosses. Jesus, abandoned in the Garden of Olives, by His Apostles, sought strength from His Father only. She wrote: "The Sisters have been biased against me, for they have been told that I would one day or other lead them into error: finally, I have suffered the most violent attacks, without in any way expecting them."

Mere Saint Joseph spoke of her afterward as the poor Superior General from whom they took away the trust of her children.

No, never shall I be able to make amends for all that Mere Julie was made to suffer on that occasion. What wranglings, what painful anxieties, what alarms of conscience did they not mete out to her, for things that time and experience have shown clearly she had no part in. . . . Our Mother loved only peace and pure faith, for which *she would have sacrificed a thousand lives*. On such occasions I have seen her weep bitterly.

But the reflection which follows reveals again her greatness of soul:

God, who was in her heart, did not delay to scatter the clouds, and He led her surely by the ways of humility and of obedience which were proper to her, without permitting that she be troubled, nor that her mouth and her heart should be lacking in any way in the duties of respect and of charity.

What was the basis of the dispute between Mere Julie and her Sisters? In the first place was the question of Julie's loyalty to her Bishop, Monseigneur Pisani de la Gaude.

It was well known that Napoleon, pretending to regulate according to his own desires the religious instruction of the people, had published a *Universal Catechism for the Empire,* where were found the "four propositions" of 1682 and other errors, called Gallicanism. Because they refused to introduce this catechism, the Bishops of Ghent and of Tournai were subjected to the hardships of exile, while Monseigneur Pisani de la Gaude went on peacefully governing his diocese. This was unpardonable in the eyes of the people, who believed that they saw therein a blameworthy condescension to the desires of Napoleon. The facts proved otherwise, but they were ignored at Ghent and Tournai. Mere Julie was included in the suspicions. They saw her completely respectful to her Bishop, whose honor and reputation she defended. Consequently, most mortifying words and actions were used against her. They succeeded in turning the Sisters of the house at Ghent against her. To keep union in her religious family Mere Julie thought she should consult M. Leo Surre, Vicar General of Monseigneur de la Broglie, to give an explanation of her conduct. But the difficulties did not cease. To this misunderstanding was added another. It referred—can one believe it—to the Rule.[1]

They accused Mere Julie of lacking firmness in the observance of the first directives given by Pere Varin.

Experience shows that this type of attack is repeated all

[1] For details see the Biography written by P. Clair, S.J., Chap. XIX.

through the history of the Church: the crisis of Purism, Jansenism, Integrism, Voluntarism, and Asceticism. Whatever they may call this passion for rigorism, this preference of the pharasaical letter against gentleness of spirit, it is completely denounced by Jesus in the Gospel; Saint Paul has led frequent struggles against the Law, the scrupulous observance of which was looked upon as more divine than charity.

A Superior, a Foundress, does not like to be accused of weakness. But when she knows that what is called weakness and laxity is on the contrary charity and wisdom, when she knows that the propagandists of inhuman austerity are under the influence of the spirit of Satan, so opposed by his pride and by his bondage to the "meek and humble" spirit of Christ, she knows that she can triumph only by humility. For in duels it is not necessary to make use of the same kind of arms which attack and wound us.

In these deplorable conflicts, Blessed Julie gave an example which all Superiors should give. How blind and incapable of government in religious communities are those purists, who ask Superiors to lead souls, Spouses of Christ, as a spiritless flock, with a rod. "On the lips of the wise man is wisdom found, and a rod in the hand of him that wanteth sense" (Prov. 10:13). Jesus did not quench the smoking wick (Matt. 12:20).

When the temptation had spent itself, the Sisters in whom Satan had inspired a certain pride of literal perfection bore witness to the wisdom of their Mother. One praised her strength of character, her simplicity, her serenity. She said: "I believe that one may say of her what Saint

Ignatius said of himself: that a quarter of an hour of prayer would console her for the loss of our houses." Another said: "In spite of the pain which this defection of several of her daughters might naturally cause her, she showed the greatest calm and she did not excuse herself in any way; having at heart the glory of God and the spread of the Institute, she used the most prudent means to make truth loved, not herself. The more I think of God, the more I am persuaded that she was animated by the Spirit of God."

This testimony is the more objective as the author, Sister Gertrude, confesses that she had yielded to the temptation of criticism, that she had been impelled no doubt by Satan, "who caught me in his net." And then she ends her confession with these words, which God permits for the encouragement of Superiors: these criticisms, "in appearance exaggerated and extraordinary, but embellished her life with the greatest virtues, virtues rare in her sex."

Thanks to the Foundress, the most cordial union has always existed among her daughters, and the spirit of the Congregation has been inspired always by the merciful virtues of the Heart of Jesus.

The death of Blessed Julie was like all the tragic hours of her life, peaceful and abandoned. She revealed more than ever the soul that one had always known: serene, conformed.

To those who sympathized with her in her sufferings, she replied, as she had always replied from the time of her suffering childhood: "God is our good Father; He is good, infinitely good, the good God!"

But this chapter which tells of her constant union with

Jesus Crucified, must engrave in our hearts the remembrance of her last days: "Under the pressure of the suffering which tortured her," one wrote, "the thought of Jesus suffering engrossed her completely." This contemplation produced in her effects like those of Saint Francis of Assisi and of Saint Philip Neri: she suffered as in a body other than her own; all her sensitivity was related to the divine object of her love, whose sufferings were more painful to her than her own. The Crucifix was her strength and her consolation. She took it in her hands, pressed it to her heart, and while looking at it, shed most abundant tears. Then, too, to obey the doctor who had ordered rest for her, she had sometimes to turn her eyes away from the holy image, as she was not able to bear—without uttering sobs and moans—the suffering impression produced by the agonizing features of the Saviour. It was not possible for her to meditate on the Passion of Jesus Christ without melting into tears. "What," she said, "a God reduced to such a state for us, for us miserable sinners!" She made them take away from her room a picture of the descent from the Cross which Mere Saint Joseph had brought to her. "My Daughter," she said, "I beg you, take away that picture: it is too painful for me to look at." All these details are pointed out in the *Process* for the Beautification.

Mere Julie died on Monday of Holy Week, April 8, 1816. The previous evening, Palm Sunday, in a gentle voice she had chanted the *Magnificat*.

We have mentioned some characteristics of the eminent virtues of Blessed Julie. And yet, many other remarkable examples of her sanctity could be pointed out. It would seem opportune, in order to characterize her spirituality, to trace the sources of this holy and fruitful life.

There are three of them which one must not omit: her fidelity to Ignatian asceticism, her devotion to the Blessed Sacrament, her devotion to the Sacred Heart.

Her fidelity to the *Exercises* and to the spiritual directions of Saint Ignatius will be more evident when we shall speak, for example, of her obedience and of her zeal. But her ardent love for Jesus Crucified is the gift which Saint Ignatius obtains for those who follow his spirituality.

From the time of the restoration of the Society of Jesus in 1814, she showed to the world her devotion to Saint Ignatius by signing her letters with these words: "Julie, known as Sister Saint Ignatius, Sister of Notre Dame, most unworthy."

On February 2, 1804, when she, with the other first Sisters, made the vows of poverty and obedience, she took the name of Sister Saint Ignatius, but she did not use it openly until the Society was restored by the Holy Father. But this mark of spiritual dependence towards the Saint and celebrated religious, evident in his virtuous conduct, and in the manner in which he governed his Order, should be recalled particularly when we speak of the love of Blessed Julie for Christ.

One of the authors of *The Spirituality of Saint Ignatius* wrote recently in an exhaustive study:

To be able to define finally the points which seem to characterize his spirituality most profoundly one must seek for the principal source of its fruitfulness . . . his passionate love of Christ . . . the enthusiasm for the incomparable Head who is

Jesus, making him embrace at once want and disgrace to conquer the world with Him, for the service and for the glory of the Father. Behold why, it seems to me, the interpreters of the Saint lead us to find the quintessence of this thought in the consecration in the "Three Degrees of Humility," to that third degree of humility which . . . stirs the soul to share fully in that which is the height of the redemptive life, the destitution and the opprobrium of the Cross.[1]

But more surely than in the writings of the most admired saints, like Saint Ignatius, one must seek the source of this love of Christ crucified *in the devotion of Mere Julie to the Blessed Sacrament*. Here the likeness with Saint Ignatius is certain, but it is equally so with many other Saints.

The spirituality of Mere Julie Billiart is completely Eucharistic. This characteristic is not casual, but essential. To make it more evident we should compare it to that of Margaret Mary, who received the greatest favors of her life before the Altar. It is said that Julie's parents had in their service a woman of about forty years of age, who was known as a solid Christian and a person of good judgment. She declared that Julie Billiart had ecstasies frequently after Holy Communion. When she went into the chapel one day where Julie was making her Thanksgiving, she declared that she saw her on her knees, her arms crossed, her eyes focused on high—facts which confirmed her conviction. No one knows how many lights were granted to Julie before the Blessed Sacrament. They tell of a sudden cure of her foot from an injury which had seemed incurable. A visit to the chapel was enough for Jesus to per-

[1] De Guibert, *La spiritualite de la Compagnie de Jesus*, p.164.

form a miracle for her such as He was wont to perform at Palestine: "The blind see, the lame walk" (Matt. 11:6).

In the Motherhouse at Namur she asked only one privilege (at that time it was a privilege): that of daily Communion. "In spite of her age and her infirmities," some one wrote, "she was kneeling in the chapel from daybreak, reciting the community prayer in a clear voice, and humbling herself for an hour, in profound contemplation before the time of Holy Communion." The fervor which consumed her soul, radiated from her face, and numerous eye witnesses have declared that they saw her in ecstasy, her forehead illumined with a supernatural light, especially during her Thanksgiving after Holy Communion.

She advised the Sisters not to speak to any one of their sufferings, but only to their Superior and to Jesus in the Blessed Sacrament. This astonishing fact was told that, when it was known that she must receive the Last Sacraments, several priests of the city asked the favor of bringing Holy Communion to her, for they knew that her fervor would penetrate them with love for the Eucharist.

Nor should it be forgotten that when she was able to swallow only a few drops of water during her last illness, "she was still able to communicate," by a sort of miracle. In that way, almost to the very end, she could receive daily the celestial nourishment which was the delight of her soul.

Why do we think that this devotion was a definite characteristic of her spirituality? Because one sees very clearly in her particular virtues the effects of the Eucharist. We have said that Blessed Julie lived specially by love and by immolation. Then, as now, what the Eucharist contains is the God of Love, Jesus immolated by Love. There, then, is the source of her love and of her self-sacrifice. In her instructions to her Daughters the Mother states this very thing with clearness:[1]

Progress in perfection depends upon Communions well made. One should ask oneself on the eve of Communion: what progress have I made in charity, in mortification, in renunciation, in union with God since my last Communion? Then one sees at once what fruit one should get from the next Communion.

The virtues proposed here are in truth those which Blessed Julie looks upon as necessary, which the Sacrament of Love produces most specially. For the word of Saint John the Precursor: "He must increase, but I must decrease," can be verified really, constantly, and fully, only if we are transformed into Jesus by Communion. And Saint John the Baptist adds the first reason for it: "He who comes from on High is above all; he who is of the earth is earthly . . . he who believes in the Son has life eternal; he who refuses to believe in the Son shall not see life" (John 3:30ff.). After Him, the Son Himself, the Word of God, will say: "He who eats My Flesh has life eternal."

It is a universal experience that few Christians believe in that infallible truth declared by Christ, the joy and the confidence in which should inundate our life. Blessed Julie had the supernatural enthusiasm which the Eucharist gives:

Oh! I beg of you in the Name of the good God (Does not that formula recall Christ's "Amen, amen, I say to you?") my dear Daughters, live always as *persons nourished by a God,*

[1] Cahier lithographie, *Themes resument les Instructions,* p.73.

who keep themselves disposed to be so nourished. Let the Holy
Eucharist become the principle and the *end* of *all* our actions.
The fruit of this life of *continual preparation* for Holy Communion, and of *thanksgiving* for this favor, will make you so
*little* that everyone will be able to trample you under foot, and
at the same time it will make you so great, so *magnanimous*
that by the strength of the good God, acting in you, you will
surmount all obstacles to procure His glory and the salvation
of souls.

We have underlined the words which make of this request of the Foundress a reflective and uncommon message.

If we were to count the hours that Blessed Julie passed,
by day and by night, at the feet of Jesus, present in the
Tabernacle, we should conclude that no one in the world
or in the religious life has spent so much time with her as
the Son of God Himself. The very frequent visits she made
to Him seemed in her eyes just as indispensable to her
daughters, spouses like herself, of Jesus immolated through
love. "As we have the happiness of making our meditations
at the foot of the holy Altar, we should enter into all the
mysteries the life of Our Lord presents, *since there Our
Lord continues His immolation.*"

It is there, in fact, in the perpetual sacrifice of the Word
Incarnate, that she saw why the Sisters of Notre Dame
should adore that Divine Presence: "Almost an infinite
number of Saints have passed the greater part of their life
there; they suffered when they had to leave the Blessed
Sacrament."

Dryness and distraction is the objection which deters
many souls, eager to visit Jesus in the chapel, so near them
sometimes, so easy of access, whilst so many duties keep

people of the world away from Him. Mother Julie replied to this when she said:

Even when one is cold and without any thought that might nourish the soul, one experiences without realizing it the influence of the Blessed Sacrament. Our Lord acts there in a much more efficacious manner than when we make our prayer in an oratory where the Blessed Sacrament is not reserved.

Filled with admiration, as she was ordinarily by the ineffable goodness of God, she cried out:

"We should be dissolved with love, with gratitude, and with respect for a God who deigns to annihilate Himself under the simple piece of bread, to nourish us, to dwell with us. Ah! how little we understand our happiness!"

She recommended to them to live with a great *desire* for the Eucharist (Mass and Communion). She loved to recite in this respect the words of the *Magnificat*. "The great desire to receive our Lord is produced by the desire to increase in the holy love of the good God." For her that was the ideal. "Recall the necessity of this desire by the words of the *Magnificat* which the Holy Virgin chants: "He hath filled the hungry with good things.""

Above all she recalled the desires of our Lord Himself:

Our Lord came into this world only after having been desired for centuries, and He is repugnant to enter a heart which in nothing satisfies His burning love and His great desire to give Himself to us, a desire which He made known to Saint Mechtilde, saying to her: "The bees cast themselves with less impetuosity on the flowers to get the honey from them, than I exert my love and desire to give myself to souls in this Sacrament of Love."

In all things Julie sees only love and immolation. At the same time they said of the Cure of Ars what one loves to recognize in Mere Julie: "The Eucharist was the passion of my life." "I should be astonished, indeed," proclaimed a pilgrim to Ars, "if it were not said that M. Le Cure lived on the Eucharist." He saw therein, as did Julie, the source of love and of sacrifice. "O my Children, what does our Lord do in the Sacrament of His Love? He has taken a human heart to love us. O Heart of Jesus! Heart of Love! If we did not love the Heart of Jesus, what, then, would we love?"

Like her the holy Cure would have wished "to have the heart of a Seraphim" and he would have wished to die of love.

The Eucharist explains the perfection of sanctity so important in Christian asceticism. The passion for poverty, humiliation, and immolation in all things does not come from a natural taste for all things which sinful humanity debases; that passion would be sterile and might become perverse. But it is born of the love of Christ Crucified who has given up His Body and shed His Blood for us—for Love only. And as the Eucharist is the Sacrament of charity, because Infinite Charity, manifested by the Sacrifice of the Mass, is given at Communion, according to our capacity, it is unquestionable that all that we have admired in the sanctity of Julie Billiart, has been derived from the Blessed Sacrament.

The Encyclical of Pius XII, *Haurietis aquas,* illumined anew the spirituality of Blessed Julie with an intense light. For it brought out with full evidence, how the love of this "God who is so good," by the gift of self in the suffering which Jesus carried to an infinite degree, was derived from those consecrated words of the Last Supper: "This is My Body delivered up for you"—"This is My Blood which is shed for you," and preceded by that extraordinary confidence of His Heart, "I have desired ardently to eat this Pasch with you before I suffer" (Luke 22:15). At the same time He shows how the Eucharist and the Cross are gifts of His Sacred Heart. "One may say," said the Holy Father, "that the Divine Eucharist, in so far as it is a Sacrament by which He immolates Himself perpetually," from the rising to the setting of the sun, and "so, too, the priests are the gifts of the Heart of Jesus." That is still more striking in His Death on the Cross:

To the unbloody gift of Himself under the species of bread and wine, our Saviour Jesus Christ has desired to add as the principal testimony of His intimate and infinite Love, the cruel sacrifice of the Cross. Thus He has given an example of that supreme charity which He proposed to His Apostles as the highest mark of love, when He said to them: "Greater love than this no man hath, that he give his life for his friends." That is why the love of Jesus Christ, Son of God, by the Sacrifice on Golgotha, reveals excellently and in a significant manner the love of God Himself: "By this we have known the love of God, that He has given His life for us. We ought also to give our life for our brethren" (John 3:16).

It is, then, to be expected that while rising from the stream of virtues of Blessed Julie to the source whence she drew this marvellous abundance of graces, one finds that it is her passion for the Blessed Sacrament, and going further, we find it is also her *devotion to the Sacred Heart of Jesus.*

This is verified not only by logical reasoning but by subsequent historical facts.

Suppress the devotion to the Sacred Heart in the spirituality of Julie Billiart and the Sisters of Notre Dame, and you have that absurd hypothesis of a river whose course would not be fed by an inexhaustible source.

There has been preserved a consecration composed by Julie in honor of the Sacred Heart, long before she became a religious. It was written by hand, July 2, 1795, at a time when consecrations were much more rare and more personal than they are today. The act composed by Julie is the same act attributed to Saint Margaret Mary: "I give and consecrate to the Sacred Heart of Our Lord Jesus, my person and my life, my actions, my sorrows, and my sufferings...."

Her biographer adds: "There is even another consecration to the Divine Heart of Jesus, written in the same hand of Mere Julie, without a date, one which the Sisters of Notre Dame preserve with filial devotion." It is relatively certain that this act was revived as of December, 1794. It has been spread through thousands of copies. Almost a century later, Cardinal Dechamps, Archbishop of Malines, enriched it with indulgences and spread it in Belgium. A remarkable point is that it contained a double vow: that of working to spread devotion to the Sacred Heart, and that of spreading faith in the Immaculate Conception of Mary. Evidently this consecration was not just a conventional gesture, but it signified a total offering of self, to belong entirely to Jesus. In July, 1795, she speaks of the Heart of Jesus, as a "sacred refuge" in which we should dwell and be united. She considers this Heart as the very holy place where one should "place in trust all our acts of charity."

It is well known how Julie was cured of paralysis in her legs which had lasted twenty-two years and which seemed permanent. Pere Enfantin had resolved with Mere Julie to ask for the cure in a Novena to the Sacred Heart; for he knew that her prayer would be specially pleasing to the Sacred Heart. This was a remarkable inspiration of Pere Enfantin: On the first day of the month of the Sacred Heart, in the midst of the Novena, he made bold to say to the paralytic, as we well recall: "Mother, if you have faith, take one step in honor of the Sacred Heart of Jesus." The command was as efficacious as that in the Gospel: "A man was lying on a bed and Jesus said simply to him: I command you, get up, take up your bed, and go into your house." Pere Enfantin forbade Mere Julie to tell of her cure. She walked and gave thanks to the Sacred Heart. This was a miracle all the more remarkable in that it inaugurated the apostolic life of her who, in the mind of God, was to be the Foundress of the Sisters of Notre Dame.

Her exhortations and her letters to her Daughters refer constantly to this chief devotion: "My Daughter, let us keep strongly united to the Divine Center of our hearts: the Heart of our good Jesus. Let us live by sacrifices in union with Him when He comes to us every day on our altars. Seek me there, my Daughter ... I sigh over the way this adorable Master is abandoned by His creatures."

The idea of reparation, inherent in the acts which we pronounce at Benediction on First Fridays of the month, filled her soul. Reparation through adoration but also through sacrifices: "Pierce with the eyes of faith the walls which separate us from Him, in order to put therein all our hearts, so that they may become victims of love and generosity towards the most lovable of Fathers."

There has been preserved another act of consecration by Blessed Julie Billiart, which concentrated on two principal ideas: she considers the Heart of Jesus is the only way to enter into the Divinity; and she asks of this Heart love of neighbor, under the form of a union like that of the Three Divine Persons. After having made to the Heart of Jesus protestations of love and fidelity, she adds:

In order to second the pious intentions of the Church and Yours, we form this holy union of which You gave us the example, O Adorable Trinity. We desire, with the help of Your grace, to work together for our sanctification, to console one another in our troubles, to warn one another with charity, to offer together our good works and our prayers, and to be animated to love You more. We unite all our actions to Yours. You Yourself, O Lord, will be the bond of this spiritual alliance which we form for Your glory alone.

Very humble petitions follow to obtain the strength to please Him even in the smallest things:

That there may be no more wilful infidelity, that all the beatings of our hearts may be a continual renewal of all these sentiments, as well as an invocation to You, O Jesus, Mary, and Joseph.

This holy union in the Heart of Jesus, made in 1795 by a small number of her companions, was destined later to be desired, sought, and petitioned by all the Sisters.

Later the Holy Father would insist on this commandment of charity towards the neighbor to which the devotion
to the Sacred Heart has given a new depth, and as it were,
the violence of an inextinguishable fire:

This devotion has for its purpose to lead us to perfection and
to the fullness of the love which *unites* us to God and to one
another while following always more cheerfully *the New Commandment* which the Divine Master left to the Apostles as a
sacred heritage when He said to them: "A new commandment
I give you, that you love one another; that as I have loved you,
so you love one another. . . . This is my commandment, that
you love one another as I have loved you" (John 13:34; 15:12).

Blessed Julie, who understood so well the desires of the
Heart of Jesus, wished that charity be one of the characteristic marks of her Institute.[1]

All these considerations, far from being as an architec-
tural ornament, exterior to the spirituality of Mere Julie
Billiart, have as their purpose and effect to show the
richness and unity of the elements of her spirituality. Apart
from this unity, one may say that each part would risk not
being seen in its true light and would appear false. The
love of God, with all the confidence that it conveys, abandonment, joy, receptivity, and childlikeness; the Cross of
Jesus with all that it requires of mortification, death to self,
abnegation, renunciation, immolation, humiliation, annihilation (renunciation); the Eucharist with all its immense
treasure of graces of union, consolation, and strength which
it encloses and which we receive in abundance with the
Body and Blood of Jesus; the devotion to the Sacred Heart,

[1] Holy Rule, Art. 5.

with the torrent of love and mercy that God has wished to
be derived from this devotion—all these factors become one
in the spirituality of the Holy Foundress. Each of them is
complemented by the others and completes the others. She
does nothing without the love of the Heart of Jesus, and
this love is in all her virtues. Yet, in giving her the gift of
His Holy Spirit, the Heart of Jesus enriched her soul with
beauty and with supernatural powers of which we must
speak to give a true picture of her soul. The Holy Father,
Pius XII, by these words urges us to do so:

"This infusion of Divine Love—sent by the Father at the
Descent of the Holy Spirit upon the Apostles—is likewise
in the Heart of Jesus, our Saviour, 'in Whom are hidden
all the treasures of wisdom and of knowledge.'" So the
Holy Father recalls in detail that there must be attributed
to the Holy Spirit the birth and the wonderful propagation
of the Church, the heroic courage of the Apostles, and that
"it is through the Holy Spirit that the virtues of the Con-
fessors have grown and that they have been incited to do
useful and remarkable things . . . that it is the Holy Spirit
finally who has led Virgins to renounce spontaneously and
joyously all sensual pleasures and to consecrate themselves
completely to their Heavenly Spouse."

He finishes his general enumeration of the gifts of the
Holy Spirit by citing the words of the Epistle to the Romans
on the love of God "to celebrate that Divine Love which
flows from *The Heart of the Incarnate Word,* and which is
infused by the Holy Spirit into the souls of all believers.

*"The Love of God has been poured forth in our hearts by the Holy Spirit who has been given to us"* (ROM. 5:5).

# 3 Temple of the Holy Spirit

To show the relationship of Blessed Julie with *the Holy Spirit* is to attempt to show the beauty of her gifts and of her virtues, the fruits of the love of the Father and of the Son. And although God alone may know the splendor of His saints, yet it is permitted us to ask Him for grace to imitate them, to penetrate into their interior spirit, that which Faith tells us to call *the Temple of the Holy Spirit*.

There is nothing in theology which reveals to us the predestination to grace and glory of each saintly individual; but there is a Marian theology which helps us, by the pinnacle of love, to find a point of comparison.

It is to the Divine Spirit that Mary owes her existence, her Immaculate Conception, her Divine Maternity, her personal union with the Word of God.

These privileges are communicated to the Saints in an analogous manner proportioned to the designs of God. Other graces, more like to those of Mary, have been granted to them. Thus, it was by the operation of the Holy Spirit that Mary conceived the Word; so it is by an operation of the same Spirit that we are united to the Word, and that we share in the divine filiation. We are really sons of the Father, Spouses of Jesus. Yet, we do not say of Mary that she is "Spouse of the Holy Spirit" by that operation of the Spirit in her virginal womb; but—and this does not lessen her greatness—that she is the "temple" or the "sanctuary" of that Spirit. By the grace of God, we may say the same of ourselves. Saint Cyril of Alexandria asks: "What is, in truth, the soul of a Saint?—A vase, filled with the Holy Spirit."

But a vase of the Holy Spirit has not the sacred and supereminent character of a *temple*. "The operation which transforms us into children of God, is only the prolongation of that which formed Jesus, the Author of grace, in the womb of Mary."[1]

Theologians explain this truth, a very fruitful one for us, that "in virtue of the intimate indwelling of each Divine Person in the two Others, the Son of God could not dwell singly in the maternal body, unless the Holy Spirit made it His very particular dwelling also."

[1] St. Leo the Great, Sermo 25 *in Nativitate Domini*, 5; P.L.: LIV, 211; Sermo 4, 206; Terrien, S.J., *La Mere de Dieu*, I, 204.

The indwelling of the Three Persons within us is not a chimera, but an unfathomable reality. If the sun has so many powerful and diverse influences on the earth and on all creation, how much more influence must the Holy Spirit have on well disposed souls who do not oppose Him by any voluntary resistance.

Then the Saints should be called the "Temples of the Holy Spirit," and, as Saint Augustine said at times, "The Mothers of Christ." The word "temple" which one most generally uses, indicated that the Presence of the Word Incarnate is sacred, but it expresses only feebly that the divine life given by Christ is the very life of baptized souls, above all those of religious souls, and still more of Foundresses of religious orders, mothers of so many souls, souls open to grace.

The temple, consecrated by baptism, by the Eucharist, and by the vows, receives more graces than the many precious stones given to the Heavenly Jerusalem, as cited in the Apocalypse (21).

The precious stones, given to Blessed Julie Billiart and to her Daughters by the Holy Spirit, are remarkable. Immediately, with the vocation of which we have spoken, she received *the gift of prayer,* an uncommon gift of prayer, flooding her whole life, and her death itself.

The Holy Spirit, the substantial bond between the Father and the Son in the Trinity, the act of reciprocal love of the Father and the Son, may be called "prayer" as He is called "Love." The soul which is dominated by the Spirit is ruled likewise by prayer; she who is not led by one is not led by the other. Habitual grace is the grace of prayer-like purity. If prayer is a raising of the soul to God, how could one separate such a grace from the Person of the Holy Spirit?

An analysis by Pere Sellier, who died in 1854, considered very exact and often cited as a reliable document, gives us this testimony:

What impressed me most in Mere Julie was her gift of a very extraordinary prayer: I believe that she had attained to a very high degree of contemplation. Before Mass, which Pere Thomas celebrated daily in her room, and during which she received Holy Communion, she passed ordinarily three hours in prayer; her recollection was so deep, that she seemed deprived of the use of her senses; she came to from this mysterious state only with effort and after having been shaken. I refer here to the time when she was confined to her bed with paralysis.

These graces appeared even at an early stage in Julie's life. Her childhood, moreover, as often happens to those whom God destines for a very deep union, as Saint Aloysius Gonzaga or Saint Therese of Lisieux was bathed in the light of the Trinity. The *Process of Information* declared: "The Holy Spirit was her first Master."

As a child she loved to retire to her little room, where, with her hands joined, she prayed fervently. The same *Process* recalled that "every day she made several visits to the Blessed Sacrament, and never failed in that program, even at the time of the busiest seasons of work in the fields."

During the twenty years of her paralysis it was astonishing to see her so peaceful and even comforted. Then, one day she admitted to Mere Saint Joseph who had asked her: "if the days did not seem very long to her, especially as she was always alone and in pain," that she did not remember ever having been weary in the eight years of her illness. If later she was weary it was because of the intrusion of a schismatic priest at Cuvilly, for then she was deprived of the sacraments. Those memories of youth had a lasting influence on the habits of prayer which spread out over her whole life.

What did the first companions who gathered around her do, without knowing God's plans for them? They prayed above all: "Around the bed of the invalid and under her direction, they prayed, they meditated together, they recited the Divine Office, interrupted by the persecution in so many monasteries, and they worked with their hands for the altar and for the poor."

The personal testimony of Pere Sellier is confirmed by the *Memoirs* of Mere Blin de Bourdon. She tells of the celebrated ecstasy of February 2, 1806. The Community had assembled in the workroom. It was the second anniversary of their First Vows. The holy Superior gave an instruction on the mystery of the day, the Purification of the Holy Virgin. Suddenly, moved by an extraordinary joy, she intoned the *Nunc dimittis*. What a surprise for all present, when at the words: *lumen ad revelationem gentium,* "her voice faltered, her eyes gazed lovingly at the Crucifix." The whole Community beheld her rapt in ecstasy . . . her body suspended above the earth, her face glowing, completely infused by a heavenly happiness. What confirmed the ascendency of the Holy Spirit during that supernatural elevation, was the light she said she received at that time. The older Sisters attested that Blessed Julie learned then that her Daughters would some day cross the ocean to bring the "light of the Revelation to the nations sleeping in death."

History has shown that God had enlightened her concerning the future during her prayer.

Prayer was for her the assured solution for all things. Evidently it was, as for all souls, the ladder of Jacob where the Angels go up and down; the direct way which leads to the Holy Trinity. But it was also light in darkness, strength under sufferings, courage in conflict, peace in temptations, mildness in struggles. In short, prayer was for her God with her, and she with God, inseparable.

Doubtless she did not look upon prayer as a childish thing. One would be very ignorant of the spiritual life to imagine that prayer is an invitation to greediness of the mind or of the senses, an appeal to joy of heart, an angelic consolation. The experience of the saints and her own experience taught her more and more each day that prayer is a gratuitous gift of God.

In the spiritual life one considers two sorts of trials: those of the contemplative life and those of the active life. Often they are mixed, as the waves and the wind. God wishes to be sought for by faith and found in charity. That is why, since she was responsible for the formation of her Daughters, the Foundress repeated to them exhortations such as these: "Oh! My good Daughters, the interior life is something so opposed to natural feelings! Do not think that it consists in sensible pleasures; no, but in mortification and annihilation of self."

This sentence should not be considered apart from all the counsels which she gave. For, as in Saint John of the Cross, the "void" that one should make in the soul—always too full of self and of creatures—is to give place completely to the "Living Flame" of the Holy Spirit. One should not define prayer by its shadow, by its negative aspect. Yet to her an ascetical effort seemed necessary to correspond to the action of grace.

This interior life in the beginning seems very arduous; one finds therein only renunciation, death to self, to one's own judgment. But as soon as one has given to the good God full freedom to act, He assists the soul which is disposed towards Him in complete generosity.

The bitterness of her trials were not sweetened, yet she does not hide the fact of her divine consolations. She adds,

I assure you, that when this step is taken, the interior life is paradise on earth. One is no longer disturbed by her faults; one knows fear no more, nor those anxieties which always try souls who reckon with God. Many act through fear. I cannot lead souls along that way; you know that is not my way.

These avowals impress upon us the constant peace in which her soul lived. This peace she derived from prayer.

She enriched her soul yet more by many other virtues in her long colloquies with God. But who can know the marvels of grace which the Holy Spirit effects in a soul given up wholly to His Love? The Hymn, *Veni Creator,* expresses it vaguely in these terms:

> Thou who art called the Paraclete,
> Best gift of God above,
> The living Spring, the living fire,
> Sweet unction and true Love.

The soul is comforted by the Paraclete. The gifts that it receives are presents from the Most High God. It is inundated and flooded by "the Living Water" at its very Source. It is inflamed by fire; the love of God envelops it; and the Spirit consecrates it to the image of Jesus, Priest and King, with the unction of the priesthood and spiritual royalty. And all this takes place outside of the senses; one possesses it only by faith.

Said Mere Julie:

If we would open the eyes of faith simply, when entering the chapel, we would feel ourselves in the place where the good God awaits us, where He looks upon us, where He offers Himself to us, His Hands filled with graces and His Heart ready to receive us. Prayer so softens the Heart of the good God that we can obtain everything from Him in prayer.

So did she plead with her Daughters to persevere in their intimate colloquies with God; and she did not hesitate to make them fear grave spiritual injuries and even the loss of their vocation, if, under whatever pretext, they should abandon this regular exercise of prayer.

To make their prayer well she counselled them to follow the directives of Saint Ignatius of Loyola. To her the Ignatian method seemed necessary—not to replace the Holy Spirit and to supply for their deficiencies—but in order to correspond better to His sanctifying action and as much as possible to offer Him an open soul, one that is humble, poor, generous, supple, ready for every sacrifice, for all favors, for all exigences. From "Indifference" to the "Election" in the *Exercises,* Saint Ignatius never ceases preparing the soul for holy abandonment, which permits the Holy Spirit to use all His "gifts" according to the plan of the Father and the needs of Redemption. Blessed Julie had understood that and she insisted on it in her directives:

How happy we are in being able to attend to our prayer life so often! There it is that we draw the Spirit of God in all its plenitude . . . the graces necessary to correspond with our holy vocation and to fill us with the spirit of our Holy Institute, which requires a virile courage, a generous heart.

And she adds more explicitly:

The fruit of prayer (and also the method of prayer which derives more and more from the fruit), is to give oneself wholly to God, leaving to Him to do with us what He wishes, as He wishes, when He wishes. Holy prayer alone teaches us how to live by God and in God.

The obstacle of which most active Religious complain, those whom the Rule calls to external work, is that of not being able to find God in everything, as one can find Him when there is opportunity to consecrate oneself to prayer entirely. To this difficulty, which cannot be denied, Mere Julie replies that it must be remedied by the spirit of faith and of love; neither one of which should ever die down to ashes.

Holy prayer is the exercise and the school of love, and there it is that fire is enkindled. For it is said of Saint Therese "that she was a victim of love, because she was unceasingly united to God in love." Yet she was not always prostrate before God in the Presence of the Blessed Sacrament, nor at the foot of the Crucifix in her cell. Oh no! She was very active; but when she conversed with creatures through necessity, she conversed at the same time with her Divine Spouse. It is an error of our imagination to believe that we cannot imitate Saint Therese, since she was not only a simple Religious, but she was responsible for much external work, even for the difficulties of foundations; and yet through it all she devoted herself to prayer. A Sister of Notre Dame must give herself to prayer, in spite of the most diverse occupations of a well filled day.

Whether she acquired this conviction from Saint Ignatius or from the Holy Spirit, one finds it repeated a hundred times in the writings of Saint Ignatius to the Scholastics during their studies, to the Coadjutor Brothers in their labors, to the professors, missionaries, and preachers. God is everywhere through His love; one should find Him everywhere through faith and through love. Prayer should be continual: "Pray without ceasing" (I Thess. 5:17).

It is consoling to think that souls profit as much from the prayer of the apostles, as do the apostles themselves. Doubtless souls receive all sorts of graces from the prayer of a contemplative who does not even know them, but perhaps they benefit more from *the prayer of an apostle to* the Heart of Jesus, in a spirit of charity. And so, very justly, Mere Julie made it a principle of education. And this principle is so readily forgotten that it is fitting to reread frequently her exhortations on this point:

It is in this union with our Lord that we learn the kind of arms necessary to succeed in that great enterprise in education, which has for its end to form Jesus Christ in the souls of children, to make them know the good God in a thorough way, and to impregnate them with His Spirit and His holy doctrine. . . . If we are not souls of prayer, we shall gain the souls of the children in appearance only. . . . As soon as they leave us, they will give up the principles they have received.

Mere Julie developed at length these supernatural thoughts, which she regarded as the fundamentals of Christian education.

Prayer not only fashioned the soul of Julie Billiart under the influence of the Holy Spirit, but her entire life was under its influence. She thought of the spiritual life only under the dependence of that Spirit of Love. She insisted on it with her daughters:

My good Daughters, do you know what is the great secret of the spiritual life? It is in keeping oneself in a continual disposition to be led by the Spirit of the good God. Let us pray that the Holy Spirit be in us the principle of all our actions. Happy, happy are those souls who are docile to the inspiration of the Holy Spirit. My Daughter, keep back that word, halt that look, mortify your own judgment, curb that natural inclination, be charitable towards all, especially towards one to whom you do not feel kindly disposed, do that which costs you most.

Then, addressing Jesus who acts always through the Holy Spirit, she adds: "My good Jesus, please do this work in my heart, for of myself I can do nothing."

It is evident that the Holy Spirit is the cause of all our sanctification, of all our virtues, of all the gifts of God, gratuitously granted to the soul through Love.

It would not be an exaggeration to say that the docility of Mere Julie to the Holy Spirit is the most striking point of her resemblance to the Immaculate Virgin, our Lady.

God cannot make us immaculate, but He has given us His Spirit, as He did to Mary. And this Spirit acts in us as in her, according to the dispositions of our souls.

The point of resemblance which impresses us most forcibly is that of *measure,* that is to say, of the watchfulness for proportion in all things, neither too much nor too little. For our passions are so fashioned that they hold us back by *"too little"* and cast us down by *"too much."* Our thoughts, imaginations, desires, projects, initiatives, wills, words, works, and even our spiritual efforts, mortifications, exercises of piety, everything, absolutely everything in us, when our self-love turns them away more or less from the purity of grace, are never perfectly conformed to the influence of the Holy Spirit, overstepping the just limits of grace, or, on the contrary paralyzing the activity of the Spirit by a certain lack of correspondence, pliability, and passivity.

Perfect docility to the Holy Spirit made the Blessed Virgin a likeness of the sanctity of Jesus Christ, without faults, without blemishes, without shadow.

Julie had understood that "the various virtues of Jesus Christ" can be in us only if each takes its "shape" in the grace of the Holy Spirit.

So, Christian mortification must be exactly what the Holy Spirit asks of each soul.[1]

In obedience one must not seek any personal advantage, but only the Will of God.[2]

Abandonment—even the word indicates—is only a "letting go" if it is not a total submission of the faculties to the inspirations of the Holy Spirit.[3] And so must all virtues be understood, not only in the observance of the Rules, not only in all the great lines of life, but in every particular circumstance.

To this effect:

Let us ask of the Holy Spirit the gifts of Counsel and of Knowledge, and let us try to walk in the Presence of God.

[1] *Themes,* p.68 ff.
[2] *Ibid.,* p.46.
[3] *Ibid.,* p.52.

When some obstacle stops us, let us raise mind and heart to the Holy Spirit and say: "O Spirit of strength and of light, triumph in me." Passions are still alive within us, so we must pray to the Holy Spirit. Without the inspiration of the Holy Spirit you will never put your finger on the dominant evil; and without the strength of the Holy Spirit you will never know how to conquer it. Tepidity in the spiritual life is not corrected without Him: it begins by a state of imperfection, by which the religious soul opposes the designs of God for her, by infidelity to the inspirations of the Holy Spirit.

Since the Holy Spirit makes of us His temples, as soon as we have been baptized, He invites us necessarily to prayer and to docility to His inspirations. It is difficult to understand how anyone can enter a Church without signing himself in the Name of the Three Divine Persons, without adoring, without praying.

## II

But a temple is always a holy place; its columns, its altar, everything that is used by the priest for the worship of God is consecrated.

The consecration of our soul results immediately from the indwelling of the Holy Spirit. It is completed and perfected by the vows of religion. That is why we cannot consider the holiness of Mere Julie Billiart without admiring the splendor of these three jewels of her religious life: poverty, chastity, and obedience.

We speak correctly when we say their splendor. For it is one thing to be poor, chaste, obedient, through the necessity of a situation, and it is another thing to be so liberally, as a man who possesses immense wealth and is prodigal of it in kindnesses to others.

What constitutes the splendor of the vows is not poverty,

chastity, and obedience, but it is primarily the vow itself, the perfect charity of the vow, the total gift of the vow, the adhesion of the whole being to God alone, the end of the consecration. And if, in the vows of religion one loves the renunciation of the goods of earth, the renunciation of the joys of marriage, finally the renunciation of one's own will, it is primarily because of the nature of the vow. It is important to take this into account when one sets out to characterize the spirituality of Mere Julie.

Saint Thomas has analyzed carefully this perfection of the vows of religion. He teaches us that they are the greatest effort of charity that we can offer to God, and that they qualify those who are baptized to carry on divine worship, with the priesthood in the Church, baptism being the first source of the priesthood of the faithful.

On the religious state Monsignor Gay wrote:

You are, then, consecrated and all is consecrated in you: your eyes, your lips, your ears, your hands, your feet, your knees, your whole body; your mind, your heart, your will, your powers, your life, your strength, your time. All is no longer yours, nor does it belong to anyone else. . . . Nothing is yours any longer; all is detached from you, sold, and delivered as a rule into the hands of the sovereign owner. You are the property of God, His own and exclusive property. Like Jesus you live for the Father, and you live only for Him, to praise Him, to magnify Him, to bless Him, to render to Him all the thousand duties which His holy perfections demand. You live to thank Him, to console Him, to make amends to Him, to love Him, to serve Him; to serve Him while working, to serve Him in suffering, to serve Him by spending yourself for Him. You live above all to *belong* to Him. In this one word there are worlds of life, of greatness, of holiness, of glory, and of bliss.[1]

[1] *Vie et vertus chretiennes*, I, 102–103.

This page from Monsignor Gay shows very well how charity, by the vow, is consummated and exclusive.

But it must be added that the vows unite our holocaust with that of Jesus: "You are victims, victims, which God the Father holds, which God the Son immolates, which God the Holy Spirit consumes, and which must be given in communion to the entire Trinity.[1]

The communion of self given to the Trinity, of which Monsignor Gay speaks, is nothing else than the transformation of our being by the fire of the Holy Spirit, in glory.

Our consecration by the vows is so profound, that it gives up to God not only the matter of the three vows, but also, in a secondary manner, but real nevertheless, all our actions done in virtue of our consecration.

At all times and in all places, for all, you are Religious. Whatever human action you perform, even if it is the most common act, that act can and ought to be sacred, and there is nothing, not even your sleep, which may not be a part of the worship you render to God.[2]

That theological reminder is very necessary to understand the meaning of these words.

Julie Billiart had a passionate love for poverty, for chastity, and for obedience. How many Religious practise their vows in a listless way, in almost an indifferent way, because they are ignorant of their supreme grandeur.

Mere Julie suffered poverty not as a sad calamity, as a hindrance to good, as an obstacle to overthrow, but she sought it as the pearl in the parable of the Gospel. She had the same sentiments as Saint Francis of Assisi who re-

[1] *Ibid.*
[2] *Ibid.*

spected poverty as his noble lady and cherished her as a spouse. Later, Saint Dominic, Saint Ignatius, Saint Vincent de Paul, all saints, all lovers of Christ, competed in love for poverty, because Jesus Himself had preferred it to all temporal advantages, to the point of dying nude on the Cross.

The story of the embarrassments and of the privations of poverty began for Julie Billiart in her early childhood. The paralysis of both her limbs was a very difficult poverty, continually productive of sufferings and humiliations. During the time of her persecution she had to change her residence at Compiegne five times; she lived like a woman "without a home," whom the police would have seized if friends had not sheltered her. Even they would keep her only for a little while, and then they would send her away. That was far different from the comfort that she had later in the houses of her Congregation. But in becoming a religious she renounced all, as did the first apostles, except her love of poverty. For this virtue did not consist in being attached to base and rough things, but in detaching herself from misery as from comfort, from a needy life as from a plentiful life, desiring to give all that she could to God and to her neighbor. Hers was an unreserved charity and a humble and grateful service. And so her religious life was not only a reduction of material existence to a minimum, but a perpetual and increasing giving away, according to the occasion, of all that she had received from the good God. For her, all came from the "good God," and went back to Him as rays of light.

Not only did she love for itself the virtue of poverty, not only did she practise it with the most severe fidelity, but she loved the poor as well, as Jesus loved them, and because

Jesus, His Mother and His Father chose poverty. Those are two complementary aspects of the vow of poverty.

Her biographer shows that she dealt with the poor in a spirit of ardent faith. So, too, did she act towards hunted priests, the hungry, prisoners, the sick, those exhausted by persecution, and towards children who were without resources and without protection, when abandoned by their families, who themselves were victims of social evils.

No one has described better in advance of the manner of Julie's living than Saint Paul when he says in paradoxes, "as having nothing and yet as possessing all things. We are considered poor, we who are yet so rich, we are considered as having nothing, yet we possess all things." (II Cor. 1:10).

Or with more precision, the Prophet Isaias:

Is not this rather the fast that I have chosen: to loose the bands of wickedness, undo the bundles that oppress, let them that are broken go free and break asunder every burden.

Deal thy bread to the hungry, and bring the needy and the harborless into thy house: when thou shalt see one naked, cover him, and despise not thy own flesh.

Then shall thy light break forth as the morning, and thy health shall speedily arise, and thy justice shall go before thy face, and the glory of the Lord shall gather thee up. Then shalt thou call, and the Lord shall hear; thou shalt cry, and He shall say: Here I am. If thou will take away the chain out of the midst of thee, and cease to stretch out the finger, and to speak that which profiteth thee not. When thou shalt pour out thy soul to the hungry, and shalt satisfy the afflicted soul, then shall thy light rise up in the darkness, and thy darkness shall be as the noonday. And the Lord will give thee rest continually, and will fill thy soul with brightness, and deliver thy bones, and thou shalt be like a watered garden, and like a fountain of water whose waters will not fail.

And the places that have been desolate for ages shalt be built in thee: thou shalt raise up the foundations of generation and generation, and thou shalt be called the repairer of fences, turning the paths into rest (Isa. 58:6–12).

This quotation is not used for the literary beauty of the prophecy. For in fact, especially during the war which invaded Belgium, Mere Julie and the Religious under her direction carried out this program of charity in poverty; they were called Repairers (*Reparatrices*) and Restorers (*Restauratrices*) of a material, moral, and spiritual civilization which war's plague had partially destroyed.

But those whom war excites to pity and to charity are rarely so watchful and generous in times of prosperity when even the unfortunate are not lacking.

For Mere Julie there was no such thing as a time of war and a time of peace. All days were days for charity, because Jesus is always poor in the members of His Mystical Body. That is why, having decided to rebuild the ruins of the Revolution by means of education, she wished only free schools during her whole life.

Doubtless poverty does not have the attraction of riches, above all at a time when science holds before the eyes commodities and the ever increasing advantages of luxury. But one cannot imagine a Julie Billiart who would not have espoused Lady Poverty forever, because faith makes the supernatural riches of that Spouse shine with a brillance far superior to gold or silver, and because charity is purer and more generous in souls who desire only to become more like Jesus Christ.

The vow of *chastity* opened to her also, as to every Religious, the treasures of the Holy Spirit, the plentitude of

which the Heart of Jesus possesses. For her there was no
question of protecting herself by this vow from marriage
or from impurity, but of becoming the perfect Spouse of
Jesus Christ. For her chastity was the exclusive love of the
Holy Trinity in the Holy Spirit; it is the most delicate fidelity of the Spouse to Christ. It is charity in its perfection:

"My good Sisters," said she, "meditate on these words of
Saint Bernard: 'Listen, My Daughter, make your own sentiments worthy of the honor which your God shows you. . . .
Remember that you are the Spouse of Jesus Christ and
close your heart to every other object.'"

Like marriage—and yet more sacred than marriage—
chastity is an indissoluble bond with Jesus Christ.

O my good Daughters, we should say with an immense joy,
with a boundless gratitude, I am a captive for Jesus Christ! He
is mine! . . . We can assure ourselves that we belong to the
good God freely and entirely. No one has forced us; we have
been captivated by the divine charms of our good Jesus. His
Love has amazed us, and we have been made His captive. . . .
Let us not dwell on that. . . . Let each day, let each hour of
our lives forge our chains closer. For a Sister of Notre Dame
never finds her chains heavy; she would like to weigh them
down more, so as to give to her Divine *Spouse* one more proof
of her love, and enter yet more into the participation of the
work of the Redemption to which her God deigns to receive
her.

One must borrow from Saint Bernard his lofty sentiments on the *Canticle of Canticles,* in order to know what
the purity of a spouse signified in the eyes of Julie Billiart,
when that Spouse is Jesus Christ, when the Holy Spirit
Himself gives His beauty to His Spouse, and finally when

the model chosen is the Immaculate Conception, Mary, full of grace. Bernard says:

In this adhesion to the Word there is more than a contract, an embrace, a total union, where the same wish, the same refusal, binds two souls in one. . . . To God honor and glory, but God does not accept them, unless seasoned with the honey of love. For Him love suffices; He is happy in Himself; He is His own reward and His own excellence. Love desires no other cause, no other fruit than Himself. He is to be the true fruit. I love because I love. I love in order to love. It is a grand thing, that love, if at least it mounts to its source, returns to its origin, and returns always to draw from its own source the waters which make its current.[1]

Perhaps one has never expressed in a more exact way the sublime grandeur of chastity than does Saint John of the Cross in this sentence, so often repeated in his writings: "Of all the movements of the soul, its sentiments, its affections, love is the only one which permits the creature to reply to his Creator, if not as equal at least as like to like."

Marriage, in its highest perfection, will never be more than a symbol of the equality and of the unity produced by the vow of chastity.

When one knows the soul of great saints, especially Julie Billiart, one is happy to say without fear of being deceived what the same Saint Bernard said of all the Spouses of the Word: "Since she is the Spouse, the Spouse of Love, how could she help loving? How could Love not be loved?"

She loved with all her strength. But her strength came from the fact that all her confidence rested in the very Love of Jesus.

[1] *Sermon* 83.

The *Canticle* says: "Who is this coming up from the desert, overflowing with joy, leaning on her Beloved?" Note that she does not mount by her own impetus, but because the Well-Beloved, on Whom she leans, draws her by His Spirit.

If she did not lean His efforts would be in vain. But with that support, she is stronger than herself, and capable of carrying all before her . . .; she controls her anger, her fear, her greed, her joy . . .; she will bring into captivity all the passions of the flesh, putting the movements of the senses under the obedience of virtue and according to reason. Everything is possible to her who leans on Him who can do all things. What confidence in these words: I can do all things in Him who strengtheneth me.[1]

Who does not see therein that admirable tranquility which we have admired in the dealings of Mere Julie with her contemporaries? Shall we say that she acquired it by temperament, from a happy equilibrium, from an energetic will? No. She got it—and this merits attention—from her vow of chastity.

Nothing so emphasizes the omnipotence of the Word, as that supreme power He confers on those who put all their hope in Him. . . . So, the soul does not presume in itself and, receiving its strength from the Word, is capable of self-mastery. . . . Having leaned on the Word, and having referred its power in virtue to the Most High, it can neither be dejected, nor deprived of its authority by any enemy force, by ruse, or by temptation.

The vow of chastity, perhaps more than the vow of poverty, gives a depth and an elevation to a spirituality,

[1] Saint Bernard, *Sermon 85.*

which nothing can replace or equal. For it opens the door which leads to the intimacies of prayer, and to the graces of union which the *Canticle* likens to a garden enclosed, where there is a spring sealed, where the air is scented with the choicest of aromas. This fruitful spring in the gardens feeds the wells of living water. The Holy Spirit is compared to the North Wind "which distills its spices" and makes these words resound: "Eat, my Friends, drink; satiate yourselves, my well-beloved."

Again, it is not the poetry of the *Canticle* which gives value to spirituality, but the superior graces of the Holy Spirit, which the *Canticle* is powerless to describe in themselves.

If the Daughters of Mere Julie are called Sisters of Notre Dame, the first reason is not only because of the affectionate devotion which the Blessed Virgin inspires, but also the assured hope, from the pure waves of divine love poured by Mary and by the Holy Spirit into souls which, like her, have made a vow of chastity.

The poverty and the chastity of the Sisters are, so to speak, under the guardianship of the vow of *obedience*, which, by itself, raises souls to the highest perfection.

Saint Ignatius has inspired the Foundress with the idea of making that virtue characteristic of her Congregation. Let us not discuss that here. It is certain that obedience was for Blessed Julie Billiart of supreme importance.

Obedience is a conformity of will and of judgment between Religious and their Superiors. But it supposes an established perfection: the conformity of the will with that of God. There is a distinction between the two stages.

Saint Teresa of Avila—like Saint Ignatius, Saint John

of the Cross, and Saint Francis de Sales—had convinced
the Foundress of the Sisters of Notre Dame, for Julie had
read her assiduously and referred often to her writings, that
the highest sanctity possible to a creature is union with
God, and that the highest possible union with God is that
of the will. For the Creator remains always a transcendent
Being, and the Spirit does not create a new infinite being
but a new "being of love," by the union of wills. Saint
Therese says in her writings concerning the most elevated
stages of prayer, as well as concerning the states of the
vilest abjection, that perfection exists, not in "interior joys,
nor in sublime ecstasies, nor in the spirit of prophecy," but
that it "consists in so conforming our will to the Will of
God that we embrace with our whole heart whatever we
think He wishes, and that we accept with the same eagerness what is bitter as what is sweet, as soon as we understand that His Majesty wishes it." She repeats it so often,
and in all her works, that one does not know which page
to choose, for they all contain the same doctrine, with the
same vigor. Let us quote for example this passage from the
Sixth Abode:

True union can be acquired very well, with the help of our
Lord, when we do our utmost towards this end, setting aside
our own will and clinging to all that is required by the Will
of God. Oh! how many there are who say and imagine that
they desire only that Divine Will and are ready to sacrifice
their life for it. . . . Then I assure you, and *I do not cease repeating,* if you are in these dispositions, you have the grace of
union; do not busy yourself with other favors, full of delights,
of which I have spoken; for that which is more precious in it is
what proceeds from that which I speak of at this moment; one
cannot obtain these favors filled with delights, if there is not a

*true* union, that is to say, if our will is not completely submissive to that of God. How much we should desire such a union!

We have noted that she calls it always a "true union"; other experiences could be deceiving.

Blessed Julie speaks with no less emphasis nor less often of the conformity of the human will with that of God. She insists everywhere on this point: in her conferences, letters, directives, and personal reflections. And this to such an extent that, in reading her rapidly, her whole spirituality seems directed to this essential commandment: "Do the Will of the good God." All virtues, all asceticism depend in truth upon grace, inseparable from predestination and from the Will of God. Her trials followed one another as the beads of the rosary, but each *Ave* ended with "Amen."

She writes to Mere Blin at Namur:

As long as the good God desires it, you will remain there; when He wishes otherwise for you, ah yes, you will go. Courageously, we shall all do His very Holy Will.

Time is a great Master; I like to let it pass, for it will teach us many things. I go on slowly from day to day. I want to wait for the good God, to look at Him, to follow Him. My heart utters only one cry: My God, what wilt Thou have me do?

Mere Blin de Bourdon, her associate, trying to reveal the depths of Julie's soul, wrote in her *Memoirs*:

Providence blessed the government of this good Mother, because she wished only the Will of God. In confidence she said that in her journeys and in everything she saw so many obvious effects of the guidance of God that she could have no anxiety about anything, that her only care and all her solicitude were to know and to do the Will of God. That was very evident: for she undertook things promptly and fearlessly, without much concern about the means to accomplish them.

Mere Blin points out unforeseen obstacles, "secondary causes," which upset all her projects. Then she adds:

No difficulty, no obscurity deterred her; it was enough for her to know the goal to which God was leading her. Her most ordinary method was to walk blindly: she kept her soul united to God, without trying to calculate or to foresee shadowy events. She awaited the indications of Providence and followed them. She said that all places were the same to her. She gave herself up completely to her task, wherever it might be, and as soon as her work there was completed, she left.

Often Mere Julie's ill health could have made her hold back, but Mere Blin says again in her *Memoirs:*

Her strength was more than natural: one may say that God gave her extraordinary strength on some occasions. Nor did she spare herself; whatever her difficulties, she set about her work.

The fact that this submission to the Will of God has been material for a book proves that the example given by the Foundress has been understood and imitated by her Daughters. Here is an example, among many, of what she used to write to her Religious:

You have been anxious to know I returned to Namur. The good God has had pity on me. I have been very tired, but that is nothing. You think correctly that I am not caring for myself, but that I am busy entirely about my God and His work. You must ask Him to make me very pleasing to Him for His greater glory and according to His Holy Will. Where could we be better than in the very Holy Will of God?

Her way of directing souls according to the Will of God must be admired; it recalls that of Saint Francis de Sales. Here is an example of it. Her first companion, Mere Blin, says again:

Our Mother is careful not to strike right and left, without sufficient advice. (These are both gifts from the Holy Spirit.) Sometimes she lets time pass in the case of tepid Religious without doing anything about them other than to prepare them, by gentle and encouraging marks of friendship, to receive more effectual warnings.

One cannot help thinking of the behavior of our Lord towards His Apostle Judas. The avowals of Mere Julie are worthy to be remembered.

She used to say sometimes to me: "It is not time to touch such a one; we shall wait for her. She said to one: "My dear Daughter, it is God who must act in your soul: it is useless to ask something of you before the proper time, for that would only disturb you. I am not worried in your regard, since it is God Himself who wants to warn you; when the moment comes, He will make you understand and He will accomplish His Holy Will in you." She used to say to me: "There are some souls whom God leads, as it were, by Himself; these have no need of human help, except obedience in general according to the Rule, and the observance of things which stem from obedience, from justice, and from prudence."

Superiors, who believe that for which they are responsible is lost, would profit much by these lights!

And so, all along the way, in all sorts of things, prosperous or calamitous, Blessed Julie united her will to the Will of God.

Saint Igatius recommended good elections, according to
certain principles set forth in the Exercises, as the primary
end of a retreat. Julie, whether she had taken them from
Saint Ignatius or not, followed the same directives:

The motives which made her so firm in her resolutions were:
that before taking them she reflected upon them while ridding
herself of every passion; never did she allow a particular inclination to influence her decision nor any repugnance to deter
her. Finally she examined the point in question in the light of
the Holy Spirit.

Is there any need, then, of speaking of her virtue of obedience? Her respect for Holy Church and for the priesthood
was equal to that which she felt for God Himself. She saw
God in everything and the Will of God in the expressed
will of her Superiors. It is certain that she gave an example
of it, as far as her office permitted, by the supernatural and
filial manner which she recommended in her conferences.

Ah! my good Daughters, if you are not above all Daughters
of obedience, you will be neither daughters of the good God,
nor mine. Sisters of Notre Dame must be known by their spirit
of obedience. . . . It is impossible to be a true Sister of Notre
Dame without obedience. . . . A person who withdraws from
holy obedience by that very fact withdraws from grace. A
Sister of Notre Dame who does not submit willingly and without reasoning to the orders of her Superiors, would do well to
note that she is not dead to herself and that she does not understand the end of her sublime mission.

One does not grow weary of hearing her repeat the same
thing. And we shall not tire in reproducing exactly her conception of spirituality, by translating her exhortations:

When we choose virtues to practise, we should determine on the virtue which corresponds best to our state of life. Then, for us, Sisters of Notre Dame, the most desirable virtue, that which ought to be the object of our efforts, and on which we should concentrate, is holy obedience. Should we have all the other virtues to an heroic degree, without obedience they would be of no worth before God. . . . Obedience is the Mother-virtue, the basis of all perfection; it is impossible to be deceived when following the path which God traces for us by the direction of our Superiors.

This principle is so important that we do not believe we are imposing on the reader, who is convinced already, by quoting again these courageous words:

From the moment that a Sister of Notre Dame is bound to God by her religious consecration she must be indifferent to all the prescriptions of obedience in her regard. What matters it what occupation she has; she knows that she is doing the Will of God, and that consequently she is promoting His glory and the salvation of souls; that should suffice; the rest is nothing before God. Today at the head, tomorrow, down; today respected by everybody, tomorrow completely forgotten, despised. What does it matter? A Sister of Notre Dame should be happy either way.

This insistence in proclaiming the primacy of obedience in her Congregation recalls that of Saint Ignatius, Saint John of the Cross, Saint Theresa, in sum, the insistence of all princes of religious asceticism.

But Blessed Julie based her doctrine, not only on the uninterrupted tradition of the saints, but on Our Blessed Lord Himself.

My dear Sisters, the life of the Sisters of Notre Dame is the kind of life which represents best the life of our Divine Saviour. The Gospel tells us above all about the obedience of our Lord. Primarily, His perfect dependence was on His Divine Father, and even on the Blessed Virgin, since He awaited the consent of Mary to become incarnate in her virginal womb. Then the Gospel sums up the thirty years of the life of our Lord in these words: "He was subject to them." Yet more, the Gospel shows us our Lord Jesus Christ, obedient even to the death of the Cross.

To follow Jesus even to these extremities is, then, a very powerful motive to practice obedience.

But does not this very imitation of Jesus Christ oblige us to obey in the most perfect manner possible? The Foundress refers to this point very often, because she did not wish in her "Holy Institute" persons who are not truly dead to themselves; she wishes "great, magnanimous souls, martyr souls." She does not hide from them its requirements:

Of these souls the good God will ask, perhaps, their hands and their feet to pierce them, after the example of their Divine Master, nailed to the Cross. If the good God gives you this grace, my dear Sisters, do not refuse; present to Him, without a word, your hands, your feet, and if necessary, your heart. There is no martyrdom more glorious than the martyrdom of obedience. It is a sign that the good God loves you very much, when He gives the grace of a calling to the martyrdom of holy obedience.

Mere Julie had received this grace, as we know, and it was not a martyrdom made easier by her ecclesiastical Superiors.

Should one think, consequently, that the Foundress asked of her Daughters a "blind" obedience, that is an obedience which sees in authority only God, and in the execution of commands, only trust in Providence? Doubtless. For it is impossible to be attached to the poor ideas of creatures and to be united to the will and consequently to the designs of God unreservedly. That would be a contradiction which Saint Ignatius made evident. "The characteristic virtue of a Sister of Notre Dame should be obedience, but," she said, "blind obedience, founded on faith."

She calls this virtue by another name, and correctly so: simplicity. For the simple look is not a twofold glance. "Simplicity of heart is a powerful means to acquire that blind obedience which has made holy Religious and which alone will make holy Sisters of Notre Dame." Then she points it out clearly:

It is simplicity which makes us love our own abjection and which makes us desire and do blindly everything commanded us, without opposition; neither asking how or why, through the intimate conviction that one has that it is the good God who commands us by the voice of Superiors, and that the good God would not deceive. Moreover, a simple soul is so convinced of her own incapacity, that she does not permit herself to examine into anything. Behold the perfect obedience to which a Sister of Notre Dame should tend.

After having sounded the depths of the perfection of obedience, the Holy Foundress took care to show its advantages, so that her Religious might desire it deeply. She emphasized the peace and the happiness of the obedient soul; like the child in the arms of its mother, she lets Providence carry her along. Her life would be sterile if she worked outside the plans of God. In the opinion of God, what assurance she has of entering Heaven, if she can say to her Judge: "I have done Your Will, I have done Your good pleasure." Trusting God to do great things she is sure of emerging from mediocrity and human weakness.

Mere Julie said humorously:

Be good-for-nothings, and the good God, who is the Creator, will do great things with those little good-for-nothings; the more we are nothings, the more the good God will glorify Himself in us and by us.

She becomes a soul of prayer, for God does the will of one who is His. She is a joy to her Superiors. She makes rapid progress in sanctity, because she has no more that "interior viper" which is secret pride; having consumed her own wishes in the fire of her love, she is the object of divine predilections. It is by obedience that we give most glory to God, because we sacrifice what is most intimate in us and most exalted, our own judgment. So no hell for such a soul: "A Sister of Notre Dame, grounded in holy obedience, will go directly to Paradise."

She is sure of it; she is not deceived.

We have spoken in this chapter of the work of the Holy Spirit. If one were to be conclusive—one is never so when one tries to describe the effects of His Love—one should speak more of the other virtues practiced by Blessed Julie, on which are based the directives preserved for her Sisters. But on the other hand many of them will be put forth in a better light when we shall show the glories of the Virgin Co-Redemptrix. Besides our purpose is not to describe a life where all the virtues shine like the stars in the heavens, but only to characterize the spirituality of her Congregation through those who have been supereminent in the sanctity of the vocation of the Sisters of Notre Dame. As there are diverse constellations in the firmament, each of which has its shape and its splendor, so in the Church there are diverse religious orders, each of which has special graces that show forth the greatness of Jesus, the Divine Model.

*"Together, with Mary, the Mother of Jesus"* (ACT 1:14).

# 4 Sister of Notre Dame

The spirituality of the Sisters of Notre Dame would not be complete if it did not have as its crown, ornament, and interior beauty, its resemblance with Mary, Virgin and Co-Redemptrix. That is why the Foundress called her Daughters, Sisters of Notre Dame.

Devotion to the Holy Virgin is not added to the religious life of the Sisters, as a chapel is annexed to a castle, which has in other respects right proportions and unity.

Everything is in the Trinity, dependent on the Father, on the Son, and on the Holy Spirit. And yet, all is Marian. Everything is Mary. Everything is from Mary, and for Mary. With Jesus, she is the unrivalled Mediatrix, the only Mediatrix, who is indispensable.

The Foundress built her sanctity and all her work on this Trinitarian foundation, where Mary, the Mother of God, occupies a spiritual place of the first class. She says that her Institute is the "The Institute of Notre Dame," that it belongs to Mary in a very particular way!" Her will cannot be more manifestly declared than in these strong words:

In order to be thoroughly penetrated with the spirit of our Holy Institute and then to become perfect in it, one need but examine with attention whence it originated, and to consider it. The same as the "Company of Jesus," of which Saint Ignatius is the Founder, which means "association with Jesus—whence it follows that one speaks of a Jesuit, having the spirit of Jesus," the power of Jesus"—so the Sisters of Notre Dame, "The Company of Mary"; so in each one should be found the spirit of Mary, the virtue of Mary, the strength of Mary, the power of Mary.

One would need to recall the whole story of the foundation, to show that it is a title of justice and of gratitude that the Sisters bear: Sisters of Notre Dame. In her conferences the Foundress kept repeating that they had been

protected in a very special manner at a time when so many people were in distress. After so great a mark of tenderness, how could a Sister of Notre Dame who knows her origin not have boundless confidence in her good Mother Mary?

And she insists, lest one forget it:

The trouble that has been endured for the founding of this Institute, from the beginning to this very day should convince us that it is the work of God. . . . The graces which God has granted to our Holy Institute, through the intercession of Mary Immaculate, show us that the good God wants to make of us the Company of Mary, that is to say, Sisters of Notre Dame.

The series of facts which one might cite in support of this would be too long to recount. Let us mention a few.

This title of "Sisters of Notre Dame," even before the foundation of her Congregation, she had chosen for the group of young girls who taught the catechism with her, when she was still a child. This devotion to Mary led her to make the vow of chastity at fourteen years of age. The Cure of the parish, M. Fournier, had noted her habit of kneeling before our Lady's altar each time she was leaving the church. This was a daily occurrence. When she decided to consecrate her Daughters to the work of education, the first article of her Rule was to give them our Lady as their patroness and their model. A true miracle, that of a public ecstasy, which took place at an assembly called to discuss catechetical education, confirmed the divine Will that her whole apostolate should be placed under the protection of Mary.

The war, of which we have spoken several times, showed in a marvellous way the trust of the Sisters in the protection of our Lady and the extraordinary interventions of their Immaculate Mother.

The *Memoirs* relate:

We had put the image of the Holy Virgin, conceived without sin, on the principal doors of the house, with a prayer to be recited every day.

"My Daughter," she wrote to the Superior of Saint Hubert, "let the rumors of war go on. We have our great Patron, our

good and tender Mother, who watches over us. . . . Trust to
her and nothing trying will happen to you."

When the French entered Fleurus on June 15, the Sisters,
half dead from fright, retired to the top of the house, and
prayed fervently. . . . Their fears redoubled when they heard
the soldiers come up the stairs. But in the moment of danger,
the very Holy Virgin came to the help of her children. The
statue of this good Mother was exposed in an open room. As
soon as the soldiers reached that spot, they stopped suddenly,
and without further ado they went down the stairs and left
the house. They had retreated before the image of her who is
terrible as an army in battle array. In thanksgiving for all the
favors granted to the city by the Blessed Virgin, an altar was
erected in the Cathedral and services were held to thank God
and the Immaculate Virgin.

A few hours before her death, the evening of Palm Sunday, "recalling doubtless the graces which God had granted
to her through her life, the Foundress began to sing softly,
in a failing voice, the *Magnificat*, which she was accustomed to recite or to sing with an uncommon devotion."

These few memories have been gathered, one may say,
as flowers in an immense garden consecrated to our Lady.
One may readily suppose that it was sparkling with lilies,
roses, and other flowers of a very pure freshness.

In this book one must show, more than acts of devotion,
the principal virtues with which the Holy Spirit specially
adorned the souls of the Sisters of Notre Dame because of
their devotion to Mary. We shall refer in brief to four outstanding virtues: humility, simplicity, charity, coredemption.

By singling out a few of course we do not imply that the
other virtues which we have mentioned as essential to the
spirituality of the Sisters of Notre Dame were not obtained
equally as graces from Mary and through her intercession,

but in the analogies of faith, there are reasons to believe
that the filial love of Mary has these four virtues as constant
rewards.

*Humility,* as every one knows, is a virtue of unfathomable depth, because the creature considers itself at an
infinite distance from God. The creature is nothingness and
sinful, except the Immaculate Virgin. Perhaps it would be
difficult for us to assess this our lowliness, if we had not
before our eyes the example of the Immaculate Mother of
God. But the Sisters of Notre Dame cannot think of themselves as the Sisters of Mary Immaculate without trying to
humble in themselves all that flatters self-love. Among all
the virtues it is humility that the Fathers have exalted most
often and most eloquently. After the Fathers, Bossuet,
amongst the greatest preachers, has glorified her with enthusiasm and admiration.[1]

But Saint Bernard is yet more incisive for Religious:

The virtue of virginity is worthy of praise, but humility is
more necessary. The first is recommended, the second, pre-
scribed. . . . Virginity is worthy of reward, humility is a require-
ment. You can be saved without virginity, but not without
humility. . . . God can accept humility which grieves for lost
virginity, but I dare say that, without humility, even the virginity of Mary would not have been agreeable to Him. . . . If
Mary had not been humble, the Holy Spirit would not have
reposed in her, and then He would not have overshadowed her.
How, without His Presence, would she have conceived of Him?[2]

It is clear, then, that in order that she might conceive of the
Holy Spirit, it was necessary as she said herself, that God look
upon the humility of His handmaid, rather than on her vir-

[1] See, e.g., *Sermon pour la fete de l'Annonciation,* III, 435 ff.
[2] *Louanges de la Vierge Marie,* 1er hom. trad., p.906 ff.

ginity. And if she found grace through her virginity, nevertheless she conceived through her humility. Whence it is evident
that even if her virginity has been agreeable to God, it is to her
humility she owes Him.

Nothing is more important than this consideration, so
strongly supported by Saint Bernard. It pulls up by the root
all hope of sanctity in a soul which has not pure humility,
without any admixture of pride. If we cannot conceive of
the gift of the Immaculate Conception, nor of that of the
Divine Maternity in a creature who is more or less proud,
what shall we say of the pretended perfection of a Religious
who is ever so little pleased with herself? It is useless to
take advantage before God of her title of "Sister of Notre
Dame" if one is not her sister in humility. This is solid
spirituality.

So Saint Bernard did not fear to apostrophize us with
these ironical words:

What do you mean, proud virgins, if you boast of your virginity and do not take care to become humble? Mary gloried
in her humility and forgot that she was a virgin. . . . The more
the extraordinary gift of chastity honors you, the more you are
to blame by soiling that honor by the mingling of your pride.
It would be better not to be a virgin than to become proud of
your virginity.

We should have to cast aside the virtues that we attributed to Blessed Julie and say that they were only the ap-
pearances of true virtue, if we could not state that her
humility surpassed them all. This we shall have to declare
again when we shall speak of her apostolic fruitfulness.

No praises given by her contemporaries to her sanctity

have been more unanimous than those concerning her humility. She was humble with the Father, the Son, and the Holy Spirit who showered graces upon her; humble with Providence which treated her as a fruitful cloud, borne away in every sense by storms; humble with the Church, with the bishops, with the clergy, humble with the most lowly of her Daughters, humble with poor people, more even than with persons honored by the world; she never let herself, as one put it, colloquially, "show the cloven hoof" by some sign of esteem for her own judgment. Her humility made her always kind, indulgent, understanding, patient, trustful, silent, submissive, brief, always gracious, under the guidance of the good God.

Julie loved to recall the lowliness of her lineage; she seemed abashed always by the attentions showered upon her, believing herself unworthy of the least attentions; in her own eyes she was only an ignorant person, incapable of being useful to anyone, and a burden to everyone.

Although she was a very shrewd Superior, reading the depths of hearts, one did not hesitate to approach her, and to confide to her one's weaknesses, because one was sure that she would humble herself, as did Jesus at the feet of the Apostles, when He washed their feet. Any soul humbled and contrite, any soul in trouble was her special concern.

How many times she has praised humility, making reflections on the beauty of Mary.

Although the Blessed Virgin may have been chosen to be the Mother of God, she never lost sight of her nothingness," said Mere Julie in one of her exhortations. What an example for the Sisters of Notre Dame! We should humble ourselves to be employed in so great a work as that of helping to save souls; for the measure of our humility is the measure of the glory that we render to God and of the fruit that we produce in souls.

She spoke to her Daughters as did Saint Bernard. A Superior less humble than she would not have been able to express herself as she did on this favorite virtue. Her exhortations repeated what our Lord always said, and then what the saints had said, even the most enlightened, as Saint Augustine and Saint Thomas Aquinas. She recommended humility to her daughters with a very particular accent of conviction:

A Sister of Notre Dame who desires to promote the glory of God, should humble and annihilate herself in the smallest things, distrusting herself extremely, so that in the big things, distrusting herself yet more, on the principle of religious humility, she trusts everything to God.

A Sister of Notre Dame who wishes to bear fruit in souls, must converse with them in sentiments of humility and of annihilation of self.

Sometimes in her words one recognizes echoes of her own life. Thus:

Let us never be troubled when it will please the Lord to heap humiliations upon us, for we may believe that we get great merit from them, and we may rejoice in the glory that the good God receives in a soul who despises herself.

Everyone could say: "That is her portrait!"

And as she wished to expect everything from the good-

ness of God, she repeated that was impossible if one ceased
to be humble; one would fall under "the sway of the
demon." She, who was so reserved in her judgments, said:

"It would be stupendous pride to rely on self . . . the
overthrow of our Holy Institute."

At the risk of wounding souls that were very sensitive,
she did not fear to give examples of religious who have
"humility with a hook," of souls who rejoice when they are
appreciated at their just value . . . as being good for nothing,
as being nothing, as deserving nothing. One cannot be a
Sister of Notre Dame without that ". . . holy humility,
without which we shall not be true Sisters of Notre Dame,
without which we cannot persevere in our vocation. . . . If
humility is necessary for every Christian, it is indispensable
for the perfection of a Sister of Notre Dame."

For Mere Julie, humility is the virtue characteristic of
our Lady and our Lord: "Let us walk courageously in the
footsteps of our Lord Jesus Christ, humble, unknown,
saving the world while trampled under its feet."

Humility, when it is not false humility, leads to *Simplicity*. For, the very effort that one makes to be humble, is
sometimes artificial, premeditated, awkward, and can lead
to a caricature of sincere self-contempt. It is not a witticism
to put simplicity in the lead in a sort of psychological hier-
archy of virtues, as a condition of true humility.

Saint Francis de Sales, Bossuet, Fenelon, among other
masters of spirituality, have discussed this with vigor. Every
virtue, obedience, charity, piety, mortification—all can be
duplicity, mixed with a certain vanity, with self-seeking
which makes them partially insincere. Mere Julie did not
ignore that, experienced as she was, and gifted with a spe-

cial discernment of spirits. And so she did not treat of simplicity only in general, but also in "the relations of the soul with God," in "its relations with Superiors," in "its relations with the Sisters," in the "vicissitudes of life," in "the apostolate in the midst of this deceitful world."[1]

The simplicity of the Holy Virgin is here the model to follow as is her humility.

Probably, without the example that Mary gives us in all the circumstances of a life that by its dignity and by the graces received was more noble, more royal, and nearer to God than that of the greatest kings, saints, or the Seraphim themselves, we should have thought that Mary might have been able, without losing her dignity, to keep her rank before God and before men, with a certain majesty. She would have been able, doubtless, without sacrificing the honor which God had done her, to use less homely things, language more select, to boast of more noble relatives, under the pretext that she was the Mother of God. And Saint Joseph, in turn, would have acted as the Son of David, as the Angel had saluted him (Matt. 1:20).

All the characteristics which Bossuet praises in the sanctity of Saint Joseph are less admirable than those of his Spouse, the Virgin Mary, who by a unique privilege could have no self-reflections, but who went straight to God, without reflection and without deviation. Peguy has sung of this absolute rectitude in the *Presentation de la Beauce a Notre Dame*. Bossuet also exalts the simplicity of the apostles, especially that of Saint Paul. He goes at once to the crux of a subject: "The discourse of the Apostle is simple but his thoughts are divine. . . . With Him Jesus

[1] *Petit Traite de perfection*, p.39, a. 55.

Christ takes first place; and His Name, which is on his lips always, His Mysteries, which he deals with so divinely, make his simplicity all powerful."[1]

The orator recalls his extraordinary power. Whence comes it?

A supernatural power which brings into relief what the proud despise is spread out and blended in the simplicity of his words. . . . It is by that divine virtue of simplicity that the Apostle has brought all things into subjection. It has overturned idols, established the Cross of Jesus, persuaded a million to die to defend the glory of it; finally in his admirable epistles, it has explained so great secrets that one has come close to the most sublime minds; after having been exercised a long time in the highest speculations into which philosophy can go, it has gone down from that vain height where they think they are, to learn to stammer humbly in the school of Jesus Christ, under the discipline of Paul. Christians, let us love the simplicity of Jesus, let us love the Gospel with its lowliness.[2]

Never did Bossuet or any other sacred orator exalt eloquence so much as simplicity. In fact, simplicity may be in itself the most powerful of human means by its virtue because it relies only on the Holy Spirit. More than any other virtue, simplicity has a large place in the exhortations of Mere Julie; whilst several spiritual subjects are treated in a few pages, simplicity, by itself, takes up twenty three long pages in her notebook. In the other seventy-six pages of the same book twenty-three other subjects are summarized.

[1] One should read in this respect the admirable sermon of Bossuet: *Panygerique de Saint Joseph,* March 19, 1661. III, 643 ff. & the *Analyse de la Simplicite,* par Fenelon (Ed. "Les Maitres de la Spiritualite chretienne," Hubier, pp.286 ff.)

[2] *Panygerique de Saint Paul,* II, pp.326 ff.

Those who are fortunate in having an opportunity to read the counsels of Blessed Julie on simplicity in her book of instructions will draw from it a profit one gleans more easily than from any other books.[1] Some excerpts, inserted here, must not deter them from reading the original.

Those who embrace the religious life in the Institute of the Sisters of Notre Dame will attain sanctity there by trying to acquire the virtue of simplicity. . . . The saints say that simplicity is nothing else than a continual act, or rather a state of pure love of God. . . . Without simplicity there is no Sister of Notre Dame. . . . It is simplicity which makes one humble; it is simplicity which makes one obedient, which makes openness of heart easier, which makes souls great and courageous. Simplicity sees the Will of God and the help of God in everything. Seeking only God, the simple soul relies on His support and she becomes strong, capable of everything, because she relies completely on God.

Is it not the example of Mary ascending Calvary which has inspired her with the idea that simplicity gives strength? In this virtue she sees also a sign of purity:

Having neither judgment nor will of her own, she is as a very pure crystal which the rays of the Sun of Justice penetrate, light, and warm. She sees therein a state of transparency of soul with her Superiors. The simple Religious seeks her peace in a sincere openness of heart towards those who guide her, and of perfect confidence in God, without need of any other help.

In order to understand well Blessed Julie's penetration of holy souls there are many beautiful, accurate, deep, deli-

[1] In the *Entretiens Spirituels de Saint Francis de Sales* to the Nuns of the Visitation there are some practical and enlightening things on Simplicity.

cate thoughts that we should cite. Let us end by this beautiful passage at least:

One of the most efficacious means for becoming simple is to strive to live in the holy Presence of God. By this fidelity of dwelling in His Presence one acquires purity of heart and one becomes simple in her whole interior and exterior conduct. The Holy Spirit watches over a soul which is attentive to the Presence of God. He is attentive to the least movements of that soul. He enlightens it, guides it, consoles it; He moderates its activity and encourages it in the work of its perfection. A soul which lives in the Presence of God is never discouraged; whatever may happen, her heart is never cast down; she never stops thinking that God sees her, that He hears her, that He looks at her, that He blesses her. This faith in the Holy Presence of God inspires her to walk with humble submission, with a masculine courage, and with a simplicity entirely simple.

We believe that Mere Julie was never more inspired than when she spoke of that virtue, so striking are her analyses and her words.

Many Christians imagine that Saint Ignatius did not have simplicity to an eminent degree, and that he inclined rather to recommend prudence. That was not Mere Julie's impression of Saint Ignatius, because she did not follow imaginary legends. She knew that great master of the spiritual life through the *Spiritual Exercises* and through the Society, which are completely revealing.

Both have taught the same doctrine on the agreement necessary between simplicity and prudence, according to the word of our Lord: "Be ye therefore wise as serpents and guileless as doves" (Matt. 10:16). One may assert without exaggeration that it is one of the greatest distinctions of Saint Ignatius that he knew how to affect a very just and faithful alliance, which is not easy, between prudence and simplicity. Spirituality has very often been exaggerated in the sense of simplicity with a quietistic tendency or in the sense of prudence with a semi-pelagian tendency. This perfect agreement is a perfection in the spiritual life, where Mere Julie has been shown to be, as it were, a daughter of Saint Ignatius, to have received the same grace as he did.

The first words written by Saint Ignatius in the *Spiritual Exercises* put simplicity as the foundation of the spiritual life. God alone, absolutely alone! No other beside Him, with Him, outside of Him. God alone praised, God alone served. The straight line, as straight as justice among all creatures, to the right or to the left, past or future, in spite of every sentiment, in spite of every reason, is the line leading from the human soul to God. Indifference to everything created is necessary to go directly to the Creator. It is the very definition of simplicity. When after a complete purification of our falsehoods, faults, deceits, betrayals, etc., we shall have become capable of choosing in all loyalty and security the Will of God, we shall have attained one of the principal ends of the *Spiritual Exercises*, that perhaps, which surpasses the others: the ability to look at life with a simple eye.

In order to gauge the importance which Saint Ignatius gives to it, we should read again the preamble for "making an election" which begins by this sentence: "In every good election, as far as it is in our power, the eye of our intention ought to be simple, considering only the end for which I have been created, to be aware of the glory of God our Lord and the salvation of my soul." For Saint Ignatius this simplicity must be progressive and, as it has been said, dynamic, urging the soul to purify itself constantly in order to seek more and more and better and better the glory of God alone. It is regrettable that we cannot quote from his writings the many reminders of his uprightness: he wishes that souls be as arrows, hurled by the Hand of the Lord.

Can one think for a moment that that is detrimental to prudence? Can one imagine that he gives himself up to a disordered mysticism, escaping from the truth of the Son, and from the inspiration of the Holy Spirit? Not a word of his expresses the fears and the anxieties of souls who are inspired by carnal prudence; it follows only the supernatural prudence which looks only at the greater glory of God, the prudence which results from the gifts of the Holy Spirit (Knowledge, Counsel, Wisdom); in his life and in his government it was carried to such a degree of perfection that there is, perhaps, no saint who can compete with him.

If this grace had not been granted likewise to Blessed Julie, whose spirituality we are trying to penetrate, we should be wrong in citing Saint Ignatius. But it seems that on this delicate point of the synthesis, it is necessary to give to the mind, heart, and soul of Julie, simplicity and prudence in all their dimensions as did the Founder of the Company of Jesus for the greater glory of God.

Saint Ignatius says on these points:

It happens sometimes that men more holy than prudent carry through a very important business project with more success than other men who are shrewder but less virtuous. The point is that the former, who seek inspiration from God in their business ventures and who place their complete trust in God are rewarded by Him, for He opens avenues of success in their ventures, in their enterprises, and blesses their efforts. Nevertheless in ordinary cases, it is a fact that to lead others, sanctity alone is incomplete, insufficient; it should be accompanied by common sense and tact.

On what concerns the service of God, those who wish to be very prudent, rarely do great and heroic things. He who draws back before slight difficulties will never achieve anything conspicuous.

At the moment we are making a decision it is well to examine if the inclination which makes us lean towards one thing rather than another proceeds purely from the love of God.

We recognize there His Will to attain to simplicity of mind and of heart. Let us recall to souls who have made the *Exercises* that there is an essential document in them that should be given special attention, the *"rules for the discernment of spirits."* It is well-known through numerous and authorized witnesses that this gift of discernment was remarkable in Mere Julie.

In all she did she acted by the light of faith, and this divine light directed all her steps, clarified all her decisions, accompanied all her words; if she had anything embarrassing to decide or to do, she did not say: "I shall think about it." Her habitual reply was: "God will tell me what to do about it." Although she was very brisk in her thinking, she was very patient while awaiting peacefully God's moments and helps from on High, which she begged for humbly. . . .

Although she entered seriously into business affairs and sought advice from those who could help her, God alone was her hope—and so this good God was always attentive to the pleas of His pious servant when she had need of Him. Raising her mind and her heart often towards her Heavenly Father, she felt herself inspired by a light, a feeling, a circumstance which came unexpectedly to her as a message from the Lord, to give her the reply she needed. Once she had made a decision, she never worried about it. That does not mean that sometimes she did not change her way of looking at some point, but she did so in peace and tranquillity, and yet I do not recall having seen her change her decisions in any important matters; it seemed that in such things she was led by interior lights which did not deceive her. Their success, often contrary to human reasoning, showed whence had come her advice (as a contemporary testified.)

Pere Ribadeneira, one of the most intimate confidants of Saint Ignatius, says that the Saint had a method of procedure which was likewise customary with the Foundress of the Sisters of Notre Dame:

When it was difficult to decide about several things on hand at once, all of which had the good of the neighbor in question, he felt it the right thing to yield the preference to those which would be of profit to a greater number, rather than to those which would serve only a few; to those sure to be successful, rather than to those doubtful of success; to those which could be undertaken without danger, rather than to those which seemed insecure; finally to those which would yield lasting fruit, rather than to those which would be transitory.

Finally, let us quote the resumé of contemporaneous witnesses, for they give a very clear picture of Blessed Julie.

To bring to completion a difficult work that he had undertaken, Ignatius summoned all the resources which his consummate prudence inspired him to make use of, acting thus as if everything depended on his efforts alone; but at the same time he depended absolutely on the help of God, counting only on Him to obtain what he required. . . . The laws of human prudence having been thus observed, he had recourse to the second means: prayer. To it he devoted long hours. . . . He appealed to our Lord with most fervent entreaties, and with copious tears, to decide what more he could do to contribute to the Glory of the Divine Majesty and to the good of the Company of Jesus. Then he had recourse to the mediation of Jesus Christ, his Divine Head, and to that of the glorious Virgin, His Mother, begging them both to do all in their power for him before the throne of God. Once after ten days of prayer before God he believed he had arrived at a decision; he was known to have taken even thirty days to reflect.

The *Little Treatise on Perfection for the Use of the Sisters of Notre Dame* remarks, as do the biographers of Saint Ignatius, that their Foundress, too, knew how to follow the counsel of the Lord, to be simple as a dove and prudent as a serpent; it adds, in accordance with the Scripture, simple as the child, prudent as an old man. "When a person lacks prudence and simplicity, one finds in her only fraud and malice."

The Holy Virgin is invoked in the Litanies as a model of prudence, wisdom, and justice, *Virgo prudentissima, Sedes Sapientiae, Speculum justitiae*: the purity and the divine maternity of Mary Immaculate are not singled out for praise, but not because the other virtues were less perfect.

We thought that we should insist first on the *humility and the simplicity* of Mere Julie, before giving to *charity for the neighbor* the eminent place that it deserves, because, in short, the imitation of the Holy Virgin is too often directed to maternal tenderness alone. Yet, one would be wrong in pretending to be "a Sister of Notre Dame," if one did not excel particularly in *charity*.

Here is a subject, worldwide in scope. It is useless to ask where Mere Julie acquired her charity. For what we have said of her filial love for the good God, of her devotion to the Sacred Heart, and of her imitation of Our Lady, has opened up before our eyes three great sources, which filled her heart with love for the neighbor.

But love of neighbor has not the same tint, one may say, according to the designs of God in all saints. For example, Saint John and Saint Paul, who were consumed with love for Jesus Christ, did not have the same kind of life. The same is true of Saint Ignatius, the martyr, and a confessor like Saint Augustine. Which has the greater love? Likewise Saint Therese and Saint Margaret Mary? They are incomparable. Was Blessed Julie filled more with the light of the Holy Spirit than was Saint Sophie Barat who lived at the same time? Pere Varin who was the spiritual director of both could not tell us. What is certain is that Mere Julie, as other privileged lovers of the Sacred Heart, had so expanded her soul, after the example of the Holy Virgin, and had so stripped herself of all egotism, in order to receive a share of that universal maternity which was so integral a part of Mary, that it would be difficult not to compare Saint Julie with the greatest souls in the history of the saints.

Mary was a Virgin and a Mother. So, too, is the "Sister of Notre Dame" through the grace of her vocation. So, too, we cannot have a correct idea of the length, breadth, and depth of the soul of Mere Julie, if we do not have a correct idea of Mary.

An enumeration of her deeds, the heroism of her devotedness, of which so many examples have been cited, do not suffice to enable us to penetrate into that abyss. Recourse must be had to Marian Theology. This teaches us that the charity of the Virgin Mother has the same source as that of her Son, that she possesses it in its fullness, so necessary is it to love all men, and sinners particularly; not all the mothers of the earth combined have ever loved their sick children in so ardent and devoted a manner as Mary. In fact, through nature Mary would have had what was necessary to love a son, but not a God. It is necessary, then, that the Eternal Father communicate His divine fruitfulness to the Mother of that Son, His Son. How necessary, O Eternal Father, it is that:

Having associated her in some way with the chaste generation through which You produce Your Word, You put into her breast some spark of that infinite love which You have for that Well-beloved Son, who is the splendor of Your Glory, and the living image of Your substance. Behold whence comes the love of Mary . . . ? It is a love which surpasses all nature, a tender love, a uniting love, because it is born of unity itself; it is a complete communication between Jesus Christ and the Holy Virgin, as there is a very perfect communication between Jesus Christ and His Father.[1]

This review of theology concerning the source of the charity of Mary was necessary in order to understand what that same theology teaches about the charity distributed to our hearts by the Holy Spirit.

There is in man a human love which comes from nature, and there is a charity which is given gratuitously by Christ. But there are not two charities, the one for God and the other for men. There is only one, identically the same; it is theological, in the same way as faith. Let us never forget

[1] Bossuet, *Pour la Compassion de la Sainte Vierge*, II, 472.

these truths: Christ loves with the charity of His human
Heart; He loves with the love of the Word, which is indivisible, from beginning to end, the love for the Father
and for men. Then theological charity is given to us by the
Spirit of Christ, which is the Spirit of the Father and of
the Son. When one loves in the Spirit of Christ, one pro-
longs without other principles the charity of His Heart; one
loves all that He loves, as He loves. It is He who loves in
us, and who attains what we love. Our act of love cannot
be cut off from its Source. It is one in its reality.

We must add that this charity is the same as that of
Mary's. That which we have just said of the love of Christ,
we must say also of the love of Mary for us. No charity is
infused without a mediator. No charity is infused without
a mediatrix. Here we do not mean a mediatrix as a passage,
an intermediary, as a crystal would be for the light. The
meaning of the word recalls the tremendous gift of self
which Mary made to Jesus through her maternity and
through her sorrowful co-redemption. Then, this gift of
self, proportioned to the plenitude of her grace and of her
merits, is the reason why we can say that our charity is her
charity, that our heart loves through her heart, that the
men whom we love are her children. If there is a continuity
in charity, Mary is after Jesus and through Jesus at the
source of all charity of the Church for men. In reality, the
whole torrent of charity by which the Church inundates
the universe is primarily that of Jesus, and secondarily that
of Mary, of the Church, of the priesthood, of the religious
life, of the holiness of the Mystical Body.

These considerations alone make clear the charity of the
saints. In some way all baptized souls participate therein.

In appearance, however, their excellences are equivocal. In the saints one sees ordinarily pure charity.

The charity of Mere Julie was as pure as the rays of the sun. And the signs of it which she showed were unquestionable. In truth, it was Mary who loved in her. Her charity was maternal, not because she was a woman, but because it was from Mary, the Mother of Jesus and the Mother of all men.

As a child charity filled her heart as the soul that dwelt in her body. Through circumstances, sick children are ordinarily egotists; they are waited upon completely when they are paralyzed. But the little Julie, immobilized, was paralyzed neither in soul nor in heart. She thought only of her family and of her companions in the village to whom she could teach the catechism and to whom she might bring gladness.

Her preference was for the sick and for the poor. She kept that preference throughout her whole life, and she communicated it to all her Religious, as a family honor, as a mark of royal blood.

"To instruct children, to keep them from sin, was her dearest recreation," wrote M. Trouvelot. Her first companions recall that "seeing Jesus Christ Himself in His suffering members, she visited the sick and poor, to whom she dispensed her little savings." Among the poor whom she served was "a little beggar to whom she gave lessons, from whom she pruned away a native coarseness, and for whom she secured a "small position." The *Memoirs* of Mere Blin abound with like examples.

Later, when her life was superlatively tormented, as a pilot on a perpetually angry sea, she had heroic occasions to practice the most generous charity. Let us cite three of them: persecution, war, the foundation of free schools.

Persecution was a period of risk, threats, and perpetual revenge. Mère Julie could have fled, so as not to be exposed to many dangers, so as not to compromise her work, her life, or her Congregation. We know persons of that type; they are conspicuous in all the persecutions of the world: Peter the Apostle before the descent of the Holy Spirit, when a servant recognized him, denied His Master. How many cowardices persecutions bring in their train. Julie Billiart, because she lived under the guidance of the Holy Spirit, on the contrary faced all dangers bravely, as did the Holy Virgin ascending Calvary. Rightly her biographer expresses it thus, when she was deprived of the help of religion: "Like the Mother of Sorrows, like Teresa of Jesus, like Madeleine de Pazzi, like Catherine of Siena, like Margaret Mary, and so many others, Julie Billiart underwent this martyrdom of heart, more painful than death itself." Her contemporaries especially admired her courageous attitude towards schismatic priests, her loyalty to faithful priests. They recall how a schismatic priest, the Abbé de la Brue of Saint Bauzille, had usurped the title of Bishop of Ghent, in order to succeed Monseigneur de Broglie who was made to pay for his apostolic steadfastness by exile. The Abbe was a violent man; he employed all means; even the most unique were acceptable to him, if he could lead priests into schism. How many were cast into prison! Among the seminarians some were imprisoned, while others were formed into a regiment. The disastrous situation for good priests was yet more aggravated by a contagious disease. Then Mère Julie became our Lady of the Refuge. She sheltered the persecuted, served as intermediary among prisoners, carried their messages, and in order to provide nourishment and peace for the prisoners deprived herself and her Religious. She sheltered those who could exercise their ministry in secret. One might relate here the same tragic story which is reproduced in all countries during periods of persecutions: Russia, China, the East and West. Communism had not yet invented the hell of violations of conscience and of savage humiliations, but unchained instincts lead always to violence. One can realize what charity asked of Mere Julie in such frightful times, when she was so completely devoted to the Church and to priests.

War was another form of suffering. War is the supreme exaltation of hatred and of love. *Life and death engage in a wonderful duel!* Mere Julie, then Superior General, had grave responsibilities. Her main concern was how she could take care of those in her charge. Her charity was stronger than all her duties; placing herself and her whole religious family in the Hands of the good God, the best of Fathers, she tried with all her strength to help the wounded and the sick. We have told before how she kept up the courage and the confidence of the Sisters who were threatened perpetually by intoxicated or enraged soldiers, by the worst of offenses to their dignity and by sacrilegious rapine. Yet fear never prevented her from opening the locked doors of the cloister. On all sides, hospitals were overfilled. Mere Julie gave generously of linen, clothes, and food. She visited the wounded, consoled and exhorted the dying. What the Sisters of Notre Dame could not do themselves, they knew how to get young girls under their influence to do.

Another form of charity which did not depend on circumstances, but on the eternal need she felt to comply with the desire of Jesus who has said: "What you do to the least of mine, that you do to Me," had always gripped Mere Julie since her youth; that is the teaching and the education of those, especially of children, who do not know Jesus Christ and who have not the means to secure instruction that they may learn to know Him and to be enriched by His benefits. As soon as she could, she opened schools for them. But as outcast children were more numerous than those who were well to do, and as devotedness without remuneration is more divine than the other, she persisted until death in opening free schools, relying on Providence for their subsistence. One may surmise, the history of free schools always raised problems at these foundations, problems of maintenance and personnel, some of which were insoluble. When free schools were decided upon, the Sisters expected from God a series of endless miracles. For often they lacked what was necessary to carry on. But the charity of Mere Julie was founded on faith in Divine Providence, and obtained the victories promised in the Gospel to faith. "Amen I say unto you, if you have faith, even as small as the mustard seed, you shall say to that mountain: Remove from there, and it will be removed, and nothing will be impossible to you." Mere Julie was one of those exceptional souls who believe, who desire, and who triumph over obstacles. Pere Varin had confidence in her virtue and he ordered her to dedicate herself to the education of youth. He sent poor and abandoned orphans to her certain that in that woman filled with God they would find a mother. Pere Varin and Mere Julie placed their attempts "under the patronage and the auspices of the Virgin Mary, offering her Son in the Temple, and immolating herself for Him." On February 2, 1804, the first three associates, Julie Billiart, Francoise Blin, and Catherine Duchatel, made the vow of chastity and that "of working with all their strength at the religious instruction of young girls." It was like wanting to walk on the water with Saint Peter. They began the work and put into it a fervor which, to quote contemporaries, would make one weep. "The rare leisure time of Mere Julie was dedicated to completing the religious instruction of the Sisters, in teaching them effective methods of teaching, in stimulating their zeal for the salvation of souls." Little by little they founded free schools. Like Saint Francis Xavier whom they had as patron, Mere Julie announced that "The Sisters of Notre Dame have just opened free schools for little girls of the vicinity." Whatever is free attracts always. More than sixty children applied the first day. As time went on the number increased.

Where had Mere Julie received her principles of education? For she had them and she gave them to her Sisters. In charity. In the Heart of Mary, educator of her Son Jesus at Nazareth.

"Mere Julie," they said, "intended that her Daughters, dedicated to Christian education, should remember that our Lady was their patron, that is, not only their protectress, but their model that they should follow and at the same time propose her to their pupils as their patron and model.

Among the Articles of the Rule of the Sisters of Notre Dame she had written this one:

To attain this end more surely, all the members of this Congregation will choose the august Queen of Heaven for their Mother, their Advocate, and their Protectress before the Lord; for this reason they shall have recourse to her with filial confidence in all their needs. Having the happiness of bearing the name of Sisters of Notre Dame, they shall strive to imitate the virtues of their august Mother.

As was to be expected, the temptation to receive paying pupils assailed the teachers. For several reasons some were received, which displeased Mere Julie very much since on principle she had forbidden it. She wrote the following letter to her little Congregation:

I beg you to receive only poor little girls who can pay nothing. I ask you to get as many of them as possible. We are at Montdidier only for the poor, *absolutely only for the poor.* If any one has charged the children, it is in spite of me. If you have one or two who pay, *send them away at once,* so that it may be seen that we do not instruct children out of self-interest. Let us not be concerned with who will feed us; our good Father who is in Heaven will care for us. If, finally, what you have is enough for two only, the good God will feed the third, or He will send her elsewhere. . . . When you see the little girls who pay tell them henceforth it will be only for those who do not pay. No matter how much you are petitioned, do not receive any paying pupils, no, none. . . . Let us go on from day to day, my good Daughters, putting the morrow into the Hands of the good God.

Such insistence is explained by a passionate charity towards the poor.

At Namur it was said that "the little girls of the working

class who flowed into the free school were the cherished portion, the flock of predilection."

Charity towards the neighbor was not limited to the personnel of her house or of her schools. It extended to all, above all to afflicted souls, the poor, the sick whom she visited, greeted, and consoled in spite of her extreme poverty. . . . When she returned from shopping for provisions, she gave a good part to the poor. When some one made a criticism on this head, she replied: "The good God will provide; this is for the poor of the good God."

"We should have the poor always," said she. "The poor are the first and principal stone in our building. The miracles in her life have all been asked, obtained, and worked in favor of the sick and the poor. And again it is difficult to tell completely the story of her charity which all the days of her life saw an increase of new and surprising deeds of mercy.

Is it difficult to think now that such a charity extended to the whole universe? How could she not have for her Daughters—and the Sisters of Notre Dame for one another —the charity of the Heart of Jesus and of the maternal Heart of Mary, whose redemption is universal?

The principle of Saint Thomas, that one shares the more in the power of the source the nearer one approaches to the source, should be applied here. The more one lives in the Hearts of Jesus and Mary, the more one's charity is like theirs, the more abundant is its effusion, the more efficacious are its effects. That is why Julie had for her Daughters the same gentleness and the same humility which the heart of Jesus has for His Spouses. Witnesses are unanimous in declaring that a visit to their Mother, a manifestation of conscience, an avowal of faults, produced in the soul not only the consolation of feeling oneself loved maternally, but the light and the courage which joy and fervor give to surmount obstacles in the religious life, and in the education of children. One might cite really astounding instances of her maternal goodness.

What she said of charity towards the neighbor she practiced. But Superiors who can say as did our Lord, "Love one another, as I have loved you," are rare, because the model which the Heart of Jesus gives on the Cross and in the Sacrament of the Eucharist surpasses infinitely all human strength. Mere Julie could say it, more than many saints. It is the advice which she gives in her conferences:

We shall never make enough sacrifices in favor of holy charity, in response to the commandment of our Lord: "Love one another as I have loved you." He gave His life for us; we can never go that far. Let us sacrifice to holy charity our self-love, our personal views, and the good God will rejoice and be glorified.

She cites another word from the Gospel:

One will recognize that you are My disciples from this mark, that you love one another. . . . I say the same to you: One will recognize that you are true Sisters of Notre Dame, holy Spouses of Jesus Christ, and my Daughters, if you have a true love for one another, if the holy virtue of fraternal charity unites us as the cement unites the stones which form a building. Our Institute is a building, erected for the greater glory of God.

Can one have a more powerful motive for charity than the word and the example of our Lord? Yes, yes, if one wishes to point out that the whole life of Jesus is that of

His Heart, for He lived and died only for love. Mere Julie derived from this Heart and from that of Mary whatever was most urgent in the practice of charity.

If we all work to make holy charity reign among us, and if we make all the sacrifices that the good God asks of us to promote the union of hearts, our Institute will be the delight of the Heart of Jesus; it will be the chosen garden of the Holy Virgin. . . . Let us ask often of the Heart of Jesus and of the Holy Heart of our Immaculate Mother, that this spirit of charity and of aloofness from the world may be kept intact among us.

It is not sufficient to ask this virtue from the Heart of Jesus; we must imitate also His generous manner of practicing it.

If our good Saviour gives us the example of all virtues, He reveals His whole Heart in the example and the exercise of holy charity, which is the most admirable expression of His adorable Heart. We must reproduce in ourselves, in all its strength, that virtue which is the Queen of the Heart of our Divine Spouse, and which is the seal on our belonging to God and on our membership in the Institute of the Sisters of Notre Dame.

The Mother adds this very important remark:

"This charity must be limited to the love which we have for one another; it must make our love as vast as the universe and destroy in it the least resentment."

She loved to suggest as models the saints in Heaven:

"By the reign of charity in it our Institute must be an image of Heaven. . . . In Heaven charity no longer costs; it is the

reward, the joy, without sacrifice; but on earth the commandment of charity implies sacrifice, forgetfulness of self, holy
abnegation."

She goes into details, so that sacrifice may not be vague:

Charity is in the disposition of the heart; universal love for
all, all our Sisters; charity in our dealings; kindness to others;
charity in keeping for ourselves the most difficult things in
order to lighten the fatigue of our Sisters; charity in our words;
never sharp and biting words; charity in supporting one another; generously upholding what might wound in mutual
intercourse, as all characters are different; helping, respecting,
loving one another.

If all Sisters were faithful to the law of charity community life would be as the life of the elect. Since we are
all the Spouses of the Heart of Jesus, why should we not
live as Spouses of that Heart?

We come now to the end of this treatise on the Spirituality of the Sisters of Notre Dame, which is the most
precious heritage of their saintly Foundress.

We have been far from forgetting the other points or
virtues of which we have not spoken and which make up
the matter of all spiritual books, such as Rodriguez, Lal-
lemant, Dom Marmion. Blessed Julie knew well the authors
of previous centuries, and one finds in her conferences
references to mortification, silence, recollection, fidelity to
grace, the good use of time, the Holy Presence of God, the
hour of death, temptation, tepidity, peace, traditional considerations and counsels, which have a double charm,
similar to that which Saint Francis de Sales had, suavity,
and that which Saint Ignatius had, practical judgment,

perfect adaptation to diverse characters and to actual circumstances. One should add that her thoughts and writings of more than a century ago have lost nothing of their value, neither theoretically nor concretely. How few modern works are so characterized?

In this limited book, however, there was not question of reproducing entirely the interior life and the exterior activity of Mere Julie Billiart, but only the most original and the most exact design possible of her spirituality. It is remarkable for its very personal aspect which, as it were, stands out clearly. But it is evident that it is marked with a double character: that of the two great masters whom we have just named, Saint Ignatius and Saint Francis de Sales. The latter is a pupil of the Jesuits and a fervent disciple of Saint Ignatius in theological and spiritual doctrine.

When Mere Julie speaks of the goodness of God, of the complete confidence and abandonment one should have in Providence, of the love for Jesus Crucified, His Passion, the Cross, and the Eucharist, of the delicate and attentive docility to the inspirations and to the motions of the Holy Spirit, which made of her soul a very pure fire, a flame gushing up as a single jet of love which reveals her virtues and the gifts of the holy Spirit, especially of her union with God through prayer and in all things, and her charity for the neighbor, one can believe that she is listening to Saint Francis de Sales himself or reading his *Treatise on the Love of God.*

But the foundation of her doctrine is primarily in the Gospel, then in Saint Ignatius. As one sees incandescent metal leave a furnace of high temperature and become a sword or a clock, sonorous and accurate, so one saw Mere

Julie leave the *Spiritual Exercises of Saint Ignatius*. Many souls make the *Exercises,* but they do not go away marked, as were Saint Francis Xavier, Blessed Claude Colombiere, and Blessed Julie, with the Ignatian imprint.

God alone; indifference for creatures, so as to reach out to God; unreserved confidence in His mercy; attachment to Jesus Christ even to the folly of the Cross; openness and constant fidelity to the Holy Spirit; daily struggle under the standard of Christ where are written these great words: poverty, humiliation, and humility; unflinching courage, and consequent heroism to follow Jesus in the scenes of the Passion, where all sins are erased, expiated, and repaired; a spirit of faith in the Church and in the Mystical Body, where each member, priests, faithful, children, and the poor, is a Presence of Jesus Christ; blind obedience to the Spouse of the Word Incarnate, Holy Church; assured and patient waiting for the Resurrection of the world, redeemed by the Blood of the Lamb; filial confidence in our Lady, our Mother and Co-redemptrix, for the triumph of the Cross and the greatest glory of God; finally, a life of contemplation and of love in union with the Father, Son, and Holy Spirit, in which the entire creation is taken up and offered to the praise and to the service of God—such are the characteristic traits of the spiritual face, the dazzling beauty on the firmament of the saints, which Blessed Julie possessed as a disciple of Saint Ignatius, as an imitator of the Virgin Mary, as the loving daughter of the Father and as the Spouse of Jesus Christ.

It remains for us to maintain one of the most striking resemblances with Saint Ignatius: his zeal for the greater glory of God, even to the ends of the earth.

*"A light of revelation to
the Gentiles . . ."* (LUKE 2:32).

# 5 Works

## I. Foundations

We cannot detail in a few pages the works of
the Sisters of Notre Dame, nor can we make
the importance and the value of their apostolate
appreciated.

Some historical highlights will arouse a desire,
perhaps, to read illustrated brochures wherein
are depicted the details of these successive
foundations.

The apostolate of the Sisters of Notre Dame
is specially achieved through the Christian education of young girls.

Before discussing the methods employed, one
should admire the divine blessings which made

of the mustard seed a great tree, extending its branches in Europe, Africa, America, Asia, and Oceania, from the year 1751 to 1959.

Fifteen houses were opened in Belgium and in France before the death of the Foundress in 1816. We cite these: Amiens in 1803; Saint Nicholas (Flandre Orientale) in 1806; Montdidier (Diocese of Amiens), Bordeaux, and Namur in 1807; Jumet, Rubempre (Diocese of Amiens), in 1808; Saint Pierre a Gand, Saint Hubert in 1807; Nouveau Bois a Gand in 1810; Henecourt-lez-Amiens in 1811; Zele (Flandre Orientale), Renneville (Diocese of Amiens) in 1813; Andenne and Gembloux in 1814; Fleurus in 1815; Brelle (Diocese of Amiens), Ambleville (Diocese of Paris).

Today Belgium has thirty-three houses, distributed in the Archdiocese of Malines and the Dioceses of Tournai, Namur, Liege, and Gand. The Sisters of Notre Dame founded a Mission in the Belgian Congo in 1894. At that time it was a question of working for the conversion of pagans and of trying to make degrading superstitions disappear among the people. In sixty years, the Sisters have organized wonderful school foundations at Kisantu, Lemfu, Ngidinga, Mpese, Kitenda, and Pelende.

From the outset the spirituality of Mere Julie guided the Religious in the choice of the people to whom they brought the Gospel: the poor, the sick, mothers of families, mothers of future priests, and their auxiliaries—the native religious—, then the older pupils. The latter were invited to retreats, days of recollection, the *Spiritual Exercises of Saint Ignatius*. In this way Ignatian asceticism, so elevated yet so practical, penetrates a little more into the Christian

life and forms an elite whose interior life and abnegation
in charity often become remarkable. The erection of a
Novitiate in Africa in 1940, and a Congregation for native
Sisters is a witness, which one finds rarely elsewhere, of
the excellent principles and methods used in the schools
in Congo. These black Sisters, true religious assimilated
by the Sisters of Notre Dame, devote themselves with
genuine success, to the education of their pupils. It is easy
to understand that the native population is very proud of
these Sisters.

ROME AND ITALY

As heirs to the devotedness of their Foundress to Holy
Church and to the Roman Pontiff, the Sisters of Notre
Dame wished to draw closer, the bonds between the Holy
See and their Congregation. In 1931 they opened a house
in the Roman *Banlieu:* Torpignattara. Besides teaching in
a school, the Sisters dedicate themselves to the teaching
of catechism at the Church, at the Patro, at the Catholic
Action centers, and at Vacation Schools.

In two country parishes, one near Monte Cassino, the
other in Ferrara, they teach primary schools, as well as
catechism classes at the Church, and at Catholic Action
Centers.

The General Chapter of 1957 voted to transfer the
*Residence of the Mother General* to Rome. The first Mass
was offered there on July 2, 1958.

CUVILLY AND FRANCE

In 1955, when, thanks to the goodness of Providence, it
was decided that the Sisters of Notre Dame would return

to France and open a house some distance from Cuvilly, a wave of joy surged through the hearts of the Sisters of the Institute in both the Old and the New World. From Orvillerssorel, where they now have a school, the daughters of Blessed Julie go regularly to Cuvilly to take charge at the Patro and to teach catechism and to pray in the Church of St. Eloi, where little Julie Billiart often prayed. They go also to the little rue de Lataule to seek the humble home where the Lord fashioned her great soul, and especially to go to the oratory erected on the foundation of the last vestige of that humble home, to draw therefrom gay courage like Julie's, to continue the work of faith and of love once carried on by "The Saint of Cuvilly." A second house was founded at Noyon in 1956.

The English Province was founded in 1846. Actually it comprises twenty houses in England, three in Scotland, and five in South Africa. These houses have been remarkable always for the initiatives taken in Education. Some great names are connected with the development of the English Province: that of Lady Petre, who received the habit at Namur in 1850, and who dedicated her entire fortune to the education of the poor. She is known under the name of Sister Mary of Saint Francis. She had a decisive influence on the founding of the first Catholic Normal School at Mount Pleasant; she was a providential instrument in entrusting to Sister Mary of St. Philip the training of future teachers. The latter was, in truth, a genius, in advance of her times, in using new methods in teaching. In ninety-five years this Normal School has trained 8,351 Catholic teachers. Numerous schools are connected with Mount Pleasant, such as "The Notre Dame Child Guidance Clinic" (Education Center for Deficient but Normal Children). Identical or similar projects were organized at Downhill, Glasgow. In 1895 a Normal School was opened for Scottish Teachers. The first Superior at Glasgow and the Director of the Normal School, known as Sister Mary of Saint Wilfrid, cousin of Sister Mary of Saint Philip, was an organizer of the first order, who created a series of flourishing schools around the Training College and the famous Notre Dame Child Guidance Clinic; and again, The Society of Saint Wilfred, for the benefit of poor churches; The Association of Catholic Women of the University of Glasgow, The Association of Catholic Nurses, etc.

The first Provincial of England was Sister Marie de Saints Anges. In the world Mary Elizabeth Townley had an immense fortune. She dedicated herself to the development of Catholic Education in England and in the Missions of South Africa and of English Rhodesia. In 1919 she founded the Novitiate and the Provincial House at Ashdown Park (Sussex).

These notes are all too brief to give an exact idea of the magnificent progress of Catholic Education in England. Our Lady has blessed the English Province abundantly, due to the generosity, devotedness, religious fervor, and fidelity of the Sisters to the spirit of Mere Julie Billiart.

In 1899 five Sisters of the English Province embarked at Southampton for Capetown. They devoted themselves with admirable generosity in the Vicariate Apostolic of Bulawayo, Bethlehem, Capetown, Johannesburg. In 1906 they founded a house at Kroonstad, in 1920 one at Chikuni, and in 1923 at Embakwe, in 1932 at Martindale and at Somerset West. Three thousand five hundred pupils follow their courses and receive a Christian Education such as we have described it in this book: devotion to the Blessed Trinity, confidence and abandonment to the goodness of the Father and to His gentle Providence, love of Christ Crucified and of the Holy Eucharist, universal charity with total forgetfulness of self, inspired by the Holy Spirit, a filial spirit in all things towards Mary. Children and Christian adults, black and white, of these South African countries, receive through the works, prayers, and sufferings of the Sisters a solid, deep, and Christian education. They have shown themselves as capable as Europeans. Some have so yielded to grace that they have become priests or religious.

An even more abundant reward has been the blessing on the work of the Sisters in *America,* ever since they arrived in the Archdiocese of Cincinnati, Ohio. Catholic and non-Catholic pupils crowded to their schools. In accordance with the request of their Mother Foundress, they opened first a school for poor children. But it became necessary to accept pupils for higher classes. In their High Schools hundreds of young girls are prepared for most diverse careers. Since 1840 it is estimated that the Sisters of Notre Dame of the Archdiocese of Cincinnati have given instruction to more than a million children. Approximately there have been 1500 religious vacations from the schools taught by the Sisters. Of this number about 150 were for Congregations other than that of the Sisters of Notre Dame of Namur. This is surely what one may call a great harvest! Crowded because of large numbers, the Province was divided. Cincinnati, the American cradle, gave birth to the Provinces of Massachusetts and Maryland. Massachusetts,

in turn, divided and a Province was founded in Connecticut. The Province of California was founded by Sisters
from Belgium in 1851, when they accompanied the intrepid
missionary, Father De Smet, en route to Oregon.

In fine, the five provinces of the United States comprise
more than 2,500 Professed Religious, 256 Novices, and
101 Postulants.

*The Mission of China*, founded by the Ohio Province,
began with great enthusiasm, but it was terribly ravaged
by wars.

Three successive wars destroyed houses, drove out the
Religious, and threw the country into the blackest misery
and the most humiliating slavery. In 1937 Japan invaded
China. Terrifying air raids and murderous attacks struck
Wuchang, where the Sisters had been installed from the
beginning. The situation was so untenable that the Sisters,
advised by their Bishop, took refuge with the Community
in Japan. Soon, however, they returned to Wuchang, and
without delay, resumed their work in the schools. But in
1941, after Pearl Harbor, a second war broke out in the
Orient. In 1943 concentration camps opened in Shangai
where there were interned 40 Priests, 2 Bishops, 50 Religious, 1000 laymen. The Sisters endured frightful physical
and moral suffering, as we now know. All humanity has
been dishonored by those tortures. The Sisters, however,
were able to return to the United States in December, 1943.
Three years later, with an admirable tenacity and a confidence worthy of Blessed Julie Billiart, for the third time they
resumed their work at the Mission at Wuchang. But soon
the Communist tide swept over China and destroyed their
missions. They were forced to return anew to America

where they await God's hour, to take up their mission work again with confidence.

*The Province of California* in the United States comprises twenty-five houses: twelve in the Archdiocese of San Francisco; two in Los Angeles; four in Monterey-Fresno; four in Sacramento; two in Seattle; and one in Portland.

In 1951 the centenary of the arrival of the Sisters of Notre Dame at San Jose was celebrated with supreme gratitude. The religious and the spiritual development of the Province had surpassed all hope. The beginnings were very poor and filled with trials. The first community at San Jose counted seven Sisters. The College at Belmont, recognized by the State in 1868, and twenty-five other schools are in charge of the Sisters of Notre Dame. They teach thirteen thousand pupils. The variety of educational projects there is extraordinary, for besides their regular teaching they provide religion classes taught by Dominican Fathers; vacation schools; spiritual formation groups, called "released time"; many types of instruction for adults; retreats and days of recollection for ladies, groups of Christian mothers, and Sodalities of the Blessed Virgin. All sorts of attempts have been made to develop Christian charity among the races, which would be too lengthy to discuss here.

*The Province of Massachusetts* in the Eastern United States, has forty-seven houses: thirty-five in the Archdiocese of Boston, five in Worcester, two in Manchester, New Hampshire. The same Province has founded five houses in Japan in the Diocese of Hiroshima, and two at Honolulu, in Hawaii.

Japan was first favored by the Sisters of Notre Dame

in 1924. During a quarter of a century the Japanese have learned to love the good God, and especially through their hymns, to love the motto of Mere Julie "Ah! He is good, the good God!" Let us note at once the astonishing fruits of this apostolate. To date, the devotedness of the Sisters to the pagans has been rewarded by three hundred baptisms; six young girls, converts, have become Sisters of Notre Dame. They made their novitiate in the United States, at Waltham, Mass. Now the Japanese Sisters make their novitiate at Tokyo. The zeal of the Sisters extends to all ranks of society, especially to the poor and to the sick in hospitals.

*Hiroshima,* the city famous as having been destroyed by the first atomic bomb, has, since 1950, a school directed by the Sisters of Notre Dame. It enjoys a special apostolic success among the pagans.

At *Honolulu,* capital of the ancient Kingdom of Hawaii, or Iles Sandwich, the beginnings were difficult. But the hardships did not lessen the zeal of the Sisters. One may guess what difficulties and obstacles must have existed because of the multiplicity of races! The first year the Sisters registered one hundred and eighty pupils: Hawaiians, Chinese, Japanese, Portuguese, Koreans, Filipinos. What a Tower of Babel where people must seek unity in faith. As elsewhere, diverse works were taken up, which succeeded beyond all expectation: Parish Mass, devotion to Our Lady of the Miraculous Medal, Society of the Holy Name of Jesus for men, Sodalities of the Holy Virgin, Altar Society and Rosary Societies for ladies, Scouts, the Parent Teacher Association, etc. The work entailed was beyond human reckoning.

The young *Province of Connecticut* was established in 1957. It has twenty-one houses, with its Novitiate at Fairfield, Conn.

The *Province of Maryland*, in the United States, comprises thirty houses: five in the Archdiocese of Philadelphia, eleven in Washington, five in Baltimore, three in Brooklyn, two in Raleigh, one in Savannah-Atlanta, one in Richmond, Charleston, and New York.

The development of these schools is truly astonishing, especially that of secondary or High Schools. Notre Dame High School of Moylan, Pennsylvania, is a part of a unique group, composed of twelve Diocesan High Schools: six for girls and six for boys. In the block, strictly united, following the same schedule for four years, are twenty-two more parochial High Schools, recognized by the State, but receiving no aid from the State. There are also numerous academies. Within the urban and suburban limits of Philadelphia the Catholic Schools in 1949–1950 taught 21,418 girls and boys. Diverse religious congregations compose the teaching staffs. For example, at the West Philadelphia Catholic Girls High School the faculty is composed of sixteen Sisters of Christian Charity, eight Sisters of Saint Francis, sixteen Sisters of the Holy Child Jesus, eighteen Sisters of the Immaculate Heart of Mary, twenty-three Sisters of Saint Joseph, six Sisters of Mercy, nine Sisters of Notre Dame. These last, as an extra-curricular program, take over the control of the French and the Spanish Departments, and the Library. It might seem that the Sisters of Notre Dame have a less important assignment than do other congregations. It would be a mistake to think thus, for they have the responsibility and the direction of many other activities.

To appreciate the fruits of their activities it is important to note what follows: Wyncote has given diplomas to 342 young girls. At Moylan, since the opening of the Diocesan High School, 3061 diplomas have been given to graduates who have gone into the world, to propagate Catholic training. More than one hundred Sisters of the Province of Maryland claim Moylan as their Alma Mater. Moreover, many other graduates have entered other religious congregations. Among all these pupils the "barrier of color" does not exist.

## II. Education

Blessed Julie Billiart, whom all the gifts of the Holy Spirit trained for contemplation, was led to undertake the work of education only through Love of the good God and to make known His Love. With great grief she had looked upon the ruins heaped up in France after the Revolution. Only if they would be reared in a Christian atmosphere could children give again faith and evangelized customs to a society that had become paganized. She wrote in 1810, "One can have no idea of the indecency and of the ignorance of the unfortunate children of this era. . . . There are among them those who made their First Communion two years ago, and *now they do not know that there is a God.*"

In her eyes education was an urgent responsibility. From the spiritual point of view she wrote, as did Saint John Chrysostom, "There is nothing greater than to train the souls and the manners of youth." She said to the class teachers: "When I see you engaged in this work you seem to me greater than all the potentates of earth. . . . Who are we to be employed in the greatest work that can be done on earth: to labor for the salvation of souls! One would have to be a God to understand the greatness of the work confided to us!"

This very concise and very incomplete account would be useless if we should not—with the help of some fundamentals—explain the spirituality which directs that education. Again we turn to the principles of Saint Ignatius. We shall be brief on this point also, for to tell the whole truth a book, filled with actual experiences, would be necessary.

Undoubtedly in the very dry enumeration which we have made, one will have been impressed by two things: 1) The religious depth resulting from so many religious vocations; 2) The extent of the skills and the projects in which the Sisters of Notre Dame have had the courage to engage, in spite of the obstacles which they had to surmount.

Education supposes a triple formation; otherwise it is neither complete nor Christian, a spiritual, moral, and an intellectual formation. In spite of its relative importance, we do not mention the physical formation. Pupils can receive this triple formation only if their teachers have received it first and know in turn how to give it.

The Sisters of Notre Dame have never neglected this preparation for their principal work, and they have made progress only in this sense according to the new findings of pedagogical sciences.

a) *The Training of Teachers*

This book has developed with care the religious discipline to which the Sisters have submitted since their novitiate which gives them habits for their whole apostolic life.

Pere Leonce Grandmaison shows that, according to Saint Paul, it is the interior life, the life in union with God, the life of prayer and of interior docility to the Holy Spirit which is the *only* source of every efficacious apostolate, because it is the condition of capacity for apostles, of atmosphere for apostolic work, of normal growth for the soul.[1] All this holds true in the case of Religious. This ensemble of virtues is not acquired in a day. The Sisters do not improvise; they study, they submit to rigid training to form and hierarchize their faculties through long years, so that they may become pure and supple instruments of Jesus Christ.

Mere Julie wished that the teachers in her Congregation should be prayerful souls. Not only did she recommend union with God for their own sanctification, but she said: "Put the good God *at the head of your class* every day of your life; be aware of your powerlessness to do any good to the souls of your children of yourselves. Grace should work; all that we do is nothing at all if the good God does not come to our assistance." And when the children were not cooperative, she did not fear to say: "It is sometimes, even very often, the fault of the teachers, *because they are not sufficiently united to God.*"

[1] Conferences on the edification of the Body of Christ.

It is very evident that one cannot train a child, and with stronger reason a youth, and finally, an adult Christian, if one does not give the example of the perfections which one should acquire. This simple word expresses almost everything. It proves that the spiritual formation of the teacher is absolutely necessary. It matters not what training obtains this result. The importance which Saint Ignatius gave to asceticism, to the correction of faults, to the particular examen, to the struggle against the disorders of the soul, heart, and will, to the discernment of spirits, to the manifestation of conscience, to spiritual direction—all were intended to give to his Jesuit sons the virtues of educators, and not only contemplatives. Prayer is not, as an exercise, the only life, although it is very necessary to every life. Mere Julie followed the same principles, and wished that her religious should be capable of showing by their own life what a Christian should be in the world and in the Church.

In a word, let us note some of these indispensable virtues. Education supposes the gift of self, and above all the gift of graces received, the gift of God within us. The teacher should exercise authority only in the name of God. The exercise of authority is salutary only if the child is stopped from being an egotistical personality, and made to recognize God, because the teacher makes him understand that by her way of commanding. But the exercise of the true and only authority is difficult, even impossible, without the interior life and the spirit of faith; for, to disappear before God, there is necessary much abnegation and a perpetual recourse to the Holy Spirit by prayer.

At the same time it requires a respect for the varied personalities whom one must educate, and this requires a total forgetfulness of one's own excellence, a profound understanding of Jesus Christ in the growth of souls and a continual adaptation to ages, characters, gifts, and destinies. One must have tried to acquire that willing plasticity so needed to understand the difficulty of the task. How many passions of underlying pride and sensuality revolt against the good of another!

The penetration of characters, of good and bad tendencies, of true or false aptitudes, of what is hereditary or personal, of that which is exterior, veneered as it were by social pressure, and of that which is identical to the soul and to the grace of God, is a gift which no book, no culture, no method, no psychological test can generate in the soul of an educator. But everything, even error, even failures, can develop a soul. If the child is an incomprehensible enigma to the teacher, the education which she wishes to give to her is only a drill, against which the child, probably, will revolt some day.

A Sister who is united to God and who invokes the Holy Spirit has more chance of being a good teacher than a person who depends upon her own ability. How many times the child foils that cleverness by turning it into ridicule.

But on one point—visible and continual unselfishness— that Sister has no rivals. It is a virtue necessary to attain the end that one has in view in education. For if Christian authority is a service, that service is continual, like maternity, when there is question of rearing a child.

Is it not superfluous to speak of devotedness? The description of it by a famous educator represents the life of a Sister of Notre Dame, such as Mere Julie Billiart would have it be.[1] Abbe Poulet wrote:

It is a question of life without freedom, without rest, without apparent glory, where one must shrink continually, control oneself, be here, there, and everywhere, renounce oneself. Extraordinary zeal and solicitude are required, a solicitude which extends to everything: to the mind of the child, to her heart, to her temperament, to her health, to her vivacity, to her progress or to her dilatoriness, to her slowness in her prayer life and in virtue, in the arts and sciences; to her relations within and without; to her qualities for developing them; to her faults in order to correct them, and at the same time supporting them with patience; to her sorrows, to her discouragements, to her worries, to her distresses, to her inexplicable fits of temper. In the subconscious modern psychology has discovered riches and obscure snares which, one day, will burst forth with force. In fine, from the most noble appetite to the humble needs, how many scales of silent notes must one know how to play!

The Sister of Notre Dame is not only ready for devotedness through her spirituality, but she desires it; she accepts all crosses as an unexpected joy, wished for, to be offered to Jesus.

What Mere Julie taught her is above all an alliance, which only the Heart of Jesus knows how to evaluate perfectly: of *confident goodness and of persevering firmness.* She whose motto was, "Ah! How good is the good God," looked upon kindness as the highest image of God. A child who does not find maternal kindness in a teacher, who does not feel confidence in her, is a child who closes up, who is

[1] Abbé Poulet, *Dupanloup: de l'education,* II.

the plaything of her feelings, who makes lying her defense; in fine, that child is lost for education. Confident kindness is lacking often in the fathers of families and even in mothers, who are excited and irritable; it is lacking, with more reason in teachers. But for a Daughter of Blessed Julie, it is a heritage of her religious family and a grace of her vocation.

Is it not, perhaps, this dominant quality which has assured their astonishing success to the Sisters of Notre Dame?

Kindness is essential to the educator; this kindness should be firm, courageous, exacting, resistant, persevering. Without kindness the teacher risks becoming dull, of becoming, under the feet of the egotistical and wilful child, mere melted snow. Julie Billiart expressed her thoughts on this: "The spirit of charity which the good God puts into the soul whom He assigns to a post, is accompanied by firmness always." One should never say of a teacher that she is too kind: we are in an age when much strength of character is needed! It is the good God who gives the happy medium, the good God who reaches His ends "gently and firmly." Firmness is a virtue of the first order, because the "common good," which dominates the individual good, can be procured for all children if one resists the allurement or the pressure of egoisms, her own first of all. Firmness resembles the bar of iron in its rigidity, but not in reality. Our Lord Himself, who never yielded an inch in the attacks on the Pharisees, was always "meek and humble of heart." Through Him the Prophecy of Isaias must be accomplished: "Behold My Servant whom I have chosen, my Well-Beloved who has all my favor. I will pour out my

Spirit upon him. . . ." And what will that Spirit be if not a spirit of gentleness?

> He will not cry out loudly nor dispute.
> No one will hear his voice on the highways.
> The bruised reed he will not break,
> and the smoking wick he will not extinguish.

The firmness of Jesus is that of unity with His Father. By doing the Will of His Father always, He has fulfilled the Scriptures, fulfilled all the prophesies concerning Him, observed the least iota of the Law: it is the firmness He showed when Peter rebelled against the Passion, the firmness when He gave Himself up in the Garden of Olives; the firmness before the tribunals, in the scourging, and the Crucifixion. In short, firmness consists in doing all good, without fear and without weakness, and in resisting evil without compromise. The teacher ought to have this firmness, or the Kingdom will not advance, because the Will of God will not be fulfilled. That does not mean that good must be done and evil avoided with the arms of Satan. "Charity, in truth, is long-suffering, obliging . . . it excuses all, it hopes all, it endures all." The teaching of Julie Billiart is but an echo of the Gospel. She derives it from the Heart of Jesus, patient and most merciful.

Good must not be sought with too much natural eagerness; that comes only from an overheated imagination which does not endure, the wind soon blows it away. . . . It must begin gently always, for that is the pace which the good God takes. . . .

Do not speak in a hard tone, but in a kindly manner say things with gentleness, and repeat them unwearyingly. . . .

Lively characters think they will do wonders by following their zealous impulses. No, no, let us listen to the inspiration of the good God, and we shall find all will be better . . . let us cool off our thoughts before speaking.[1]

But this charity is possible only if the soul has been prepared by the spirit of love to forget self completely, and to think only and to desire only God. Thus one goes back always to the same principle: The education of children and of adults is a difficult task, liable to many illusions, errors, and cowardices, if the educator is not a saint, or at least if she is not trying to become one by an interior life, such as we have described in this book.

Many sacrifices are necessary, however, of which we have not time to speak here, such as that of obedience, to undertake an assignment more or less austere or unforeseen, to acquire the knowledge necessary for teaching and for acquiring degrees, to live in a country where an unfamiliar language is spoken and whose climate tries one's health, and to endure other very hard things sometimes. Such sacrifices have been asked of religious of very high virtue, but such souls need the graces of a very special vocation.

b) *The Training of Young Girls*

The educator must attain four or five ends at least: acquisition of knowledge, development of the faculties, especially that of the will, desirable qualities of heart, preparation for marriage and for family life, social and apostolic activity.

Over and above these immediate ends, dominating them

[1] *Letters to Her Daughters.*

all, explaining and directing them, there is necessary the principal end which Blessed Julie stressed: *The glory of God* and then *the sanctification of souls.*

She insisted more, perhaps, on Christian training in "the goodness of God, in what our Lord Jesus Christ had done for the salvation of souls"—on "the sorrow we must have for having offended so good a God." The dogma of the Love of God was in her mind the burden of all teaching.

The eve of her death, Julie sent to her Daughters the following recommendations: "Tell them that I bless them and that I recommend to them to say always, in all the events of life: "How good is the good God!" There should be no multiplying of religious practices, but a constant referring to God the Father, to the Son, and to the Holy Spirit. A fervent devotion to the spirit of charity in all things should penetrate their whole life and imprint there the seal of true Christianity." "Shape souls according to the Gospel," she would repeat, "and you will make souls greater."

The Eucharist and a filial devotion to Our Lady were in her eyes the great means of sanctification.

She did not forget that education should aim to form the whole of the human person, and she wished that her daughters should work at that with all their strength.

The simple enumeration of the diverse ends of education resemble the conquest of five different worlds, as Europe, Asia, America, etc. Should we enter any one of these areas we should see that the education of a young girl requires many types of teachers: the father, the mother, diverse technicians, apprenticeships directed and controlled in specialized surroundings, etc. What do we expect consequently from a Sister of Notre Dame? Assuredly knowledge, culture, experience, but above all spirituality, proper to lead these multiple programs according to the surest and most efficacious Christian spirit. For it is worth little to have a vigorous body, if the soul which directs the body has neither intelligence, nor memory, nor energy. Moreover, what does it profit a soul, said Our Lord, to gain the whole world if one loses his soul, and even makes others lose theirs?

It is an evident truth for the Sisters of Notre Dame as well as for all Christian educators, that Christianity should penetrate all types of activity, and that without Christianity pagan philosophy or any passion will precipitate the soul down the slope which leads to misfortune or perhaps to damnation. No educator in Notre Dame has ever imagined that the Christian life is a life separated from the human, conjugal, family, and social life. If she did, the Christian would be at once a son of God by Baptism and a pagan by customs, which is monstrous. But what problems do present themselves to a teacher! This is not the place to state nor to solve such problems. We wish merely to remark that a spirit and a love that are but mediocre cannot face up to the trials of this life, terrible as they are sometimes, and they sink in the tempest, as a ship which is not balanced but liable to the inroads of water.

Christians who are saved and who save others, spreading around them conquering example and zeal, are those only whose faith, hope, and charity, devotion to the Father, to Jesus Crucified, to the Eucharist, to the Holy Spirit, to the Holy Virgin, abnegation, humility, love of the neighbor

have, as it were, been deeply rooted in souls through education, through habits and graces which call for a seriously
Christian training.

We remarked at the beginning of this fifth part, the
amplitude of the tasks which the Sisters of Notre Dame
have undertaken everywhere, from primary schools to universities. This very extension of the apostolate is in accordance with their holy ambition to procure "the great
glory of God," but it raises new difficulties weighting down
the responsibilities of the Congregation.

One can count at least three stages in education; one
might even say that one could raise in each being three
successive persons: that of infancy, that of adolescence,
and that of adulthood. We omit that difficult age of
"Alumnae" who, in the world, prepare for their career, for
their marriage, for their womanhood.

Religious know children better than we ca·¹ say—their
instincts, their tastes, their faults, their piety, ·heir conscience. It would seem that their experience is aln. st that
of a mother of an enlightened family; but it is more extended than that of a mother, because of the multiplicity
of natures, new ones each year, that must be studied, followed, directed, and prepared for the great duties of Christian life. Children must be taught the Catechism to give
them good Christian habits. Who does not know today how
many mistakes one may make on those two points alone?
There is no doubt about it, there exist false explanations of
dogmas, of morals, of devotions, of Christian practice, of
virtue, which leave indelible marks on the consciences of
children, and which are very deadly in maturity. For example, the soul of a child can become scrupulous through

misguidance of a teacher, and never recover from that malady. One might cite many cases, where faults in Christian boys and girls arose in faulty education, and because the permanence of impressions made at time of early childhood are indelible. That is why one is deceived in imagining that one can confide children to persons who lack good sense, uprightness, truth, pure faith, exact knowledge, etc. The Sisters know this; they do not believe that their long religious formation is superfluous, when there is question of training little children.

It is yet more necessary when there is question not of raising a child, supple and pliable, but an *adolescent* who is acquiring a new personality, ordinarily intractable and individualistic. It is a great blunder, which parents blindly commit often, to treat a young girl of thirteen or fourteen years as if she is still eight or nine years, and to impose on her the same discipline, the same methods. But parents have not the experience of religious, who have both children and adolescents to train in great numbers, and different groups each year. They know from their own training, and every day they learn from facts, that adolescence is a physical, an intellectual, and a moral transformation for each child, a transformation which is not superficial, but which renews the entire being. The adolescent learns little by little that her body is not the same, that the family is not simple, that problems are ahead for her future, that her faith is obscure, that her devotion stems from sentiment. It is important for the educator not to appear surprised, and not to look upon adolescence as an ungrateful age—even if it is so in reality—incomprehensible, where everything is at fault, where there is deformation, maliciousness of character, a change from good to worst, from pure to impure. Charity makes the truth clear: adolescence is an age richer than the preceding in forces and in positive qualities, which seek only to blossom and to be harmonized. The young girl seeks to be independent of restraints, and she feels the need of independent thought, not through others but by herself, following up her impressions, her views, and her own rhythm. And as she is still instinctive, she deceives herself often, exaggerating many things, reversing what she calls prejudices, believing herself more enlightened than older persons. And all this offends inexperienced educators.

Adolescence discovers her new interior life as an unknown land which seems to her, either sunny, if she has an optimistic temperament, or gloomy if she has a pessimistic temperament. Surely the education of an adolescent is difficult and requires much confidence, sympathy, patience, energy, and perspicacity. For the young of that age wishes to find all that in her teacher. She wants to be self-reliant since she is no longer a child; but she desires, without admitting it, to lean on her teacher, because she does feel her own personal helplessness. She is too full of contradictions and of rebellion sometimes not to need someone. She is not adjusted to life yet, for life is too big and too difficult for her at that age. Her tastes, her preferences, her instincts are in quest of novelties which impress her but which she does not dominate. The great problem of undecided, uncertain love, where the ideal takes an immoderate place, envelops her soul, her dreams, her sleeplessness, her successes.

With these instincts of conquest and of domination,

instincts of defense declare themselves, as if society, the family, the boarding school authority, and tradition menaced her personality. Adolescents, also, when they do not feel confidence in others—and they do distrust people quickly—are often reticent, secretive, hurt over trivialities.

At that time religious education is not easier than moral education. For faith itself begins to be in peril. And if at that time they do not get solid principles, faith is lost. How is the Christian religion to be presented to adolescents? Certainly through the aspects which favor the blossoming out of nature, according to God and according to His grace. There are some theses on abnegation and mortification which, if poorly presented, are false and do great harm. Christianity is one; it is a synthesis; it is death and life, the Cross and Resurrection. It is God, like God Himself. Let us say that a religious who is not well-grounded in her religion and who does not know Christian asceticism except under a petty and depressing aspect would not be the right one to train adolescents. Whence the necessity of a spirituality full of light and love, like that which Julie Billiart has handed down to us.

The Sisters of Notre Dame have been in charge also of *young women adults*. New problems are bound to arise in that realm, which they must solve by supernatural means. The thoughts of adolescents are in two channels, because nature itself orients them that way: the thought of marriage, a religious vocation, and social dedication. But charity must be the motivation of the education for any one of the three: to live for others and not for self. The Sisters of Notre Dame are well equipped by their very spirituality to give that type of education. By their example they are likewise prepared to give such training. If in passing we have stated that in all the countries where they have opened schools and other projects, they have fostered religious vocations, the principal reason is, doubtless, their example.

### III. Notre Dame Education at the College Level in the United States

The opening of the twentieth century saw an awakening interest in the United States in Catholic education for women. At that time Sister Provincial Julia was alerted to the need for action on this point by officers of the Catholic University of America, who, with the advice of Cardinal Gibbons, urged Sister Julia to open a college for women near the campus of the Catholic University at Washington. For her it was a bold venture, a challenge. But her courage, her faith, and her keen vision sent her forward on a difficult journey to the day of the opening of Trinity College, in 1900. Trinity, the pioneer Catholic College of Liberal Arts for Women in America, has more than justified the confidence placed in her. Today, in the shadow of the Catholic University of America, a large campus, dotted with superb buildings, stands Trinity College, prosperous, with a large student body from all parts of America and foreign countries, and with a faculty prepared to the ultimate—an honor to Catholic education for women in America.

In 1919, Cardinal O'Connell, alert to the educational needs of his vast Archdiocese, encouraged the Sisters of Notre Dame to start a college for women, the first of its kind in Catholic New England. It was a difficult time for such a venture, just at the close of World War I; it was an area that boasted of large, heavily endowed secular colleges, which were sure to be competitors. Yet, with the courage that faith sponsors, with a zeal that would try to move mountains to give Catholic higher education to the many Notre Dame graduates of the Catholic high schools and academies in the vicinity, the Sisters of Notre Dame of the New England Province forged ahead. Today seven most attractive buildings stand on an extensive campus in the heart of Boston. A student body of more than one thousand students is indicative of the confidence of the Boston public in the success of Emmanuel College. God has rewarded the faith of the pioneer Sisters of Emmanuel College.

In California, in 1851, a charter was issued to the Sisters of Notre Dame to open a college. For many years it enjoyed an excellent reputation as a Junior College. In 1950 it was expanded into a Senior Liberal Arts College. New buildings of great beauty have been erected on the magnificent campus at Belmont, while an increased faculty and a large student body attest that Catholic education for women at Belmont is at its peak.

In 1950, the Orient found the Sisters of Notre Dame striving to make higher education a reality for the Japanese women seeking intellectual advancement. At Okayama an expanded building program, and a student body of over nine hundred provide the setting; the offerings of generous minded friends in Massachusetts provided the means to make this project a reality. In Hiroshima a Junior College was opened in 1961, to meet the needs and the demands of the times in Southern Japan.

In a word, Catholic higher education for women has been championed by the Sisters of Notre Dame in America, as in Europe. The seed, sown through the last sixty years, has borne fruit a hundredfold!

# Epilogue

The Sisters of Notre Dame who know their Blessed Mere Julie well will not be surprised that, in concluding this study, we apply sincerely to them the words that the Holy Father Pius XII said of the Society of Jesus, that was formed by the *Exercises*. These words are taken from a letter to the Very Reverend Father General, on the occasion of the fourth centenary of the death of Saint Ignatius. We quote it particularly in order to show how the apostolate is, like sanctity, the fruit of that spirituality.

The *Exercises* led him (Saint Ignatius) to side with the Divine King, worn out with pain, rent with outrages and tortured unto death, to serve His Eternal Father, to follow Him to the summit of love; to desire in the fervor of divine charity which devoured him, not only to come himself to the feet of Christ, his Saviour, but to lead the *whole world* there.

That is exactly the thought that the Foundress of the Sisters of Notre Dame had:

From the Mount of Olives resounded the cry, you will be My witnesses . . . even to the ends of the earth. If you want to love Christ, wrote Saint Augustine, extend your charity to the whole earth, for the members of Christ are spread over the whole earth.[1]

Ignatius himself saw more than a thousand companions fight under the standard of the Cross, even in the far away regions of Europe, America, India, and Ethiopia. That was the beginning of the apostolate which was to call his sons into the immense vineyard of the Lord: some to the infidels in missions that the Sovereign Pontiffs in the course of time will confide to them so that they may make an exact doctrine spread, by their hard labor and by the blood of martyrs; others to be with the heads of nations or with those subjected to slavery; others in the schools or as professors in the universities. It is to the Constitutions that he will turn to find the way by which the whole body and each of its members scattered over the whole earth, but united among themselves and with their General, by a love of the Eternal Father, will be able to realize "the ideal of a

[1] Epistle of Saint John to the Parthians, X, 8.

perfect life, which *par excellence* is the fruit of the *Exercises.*"

Is not this letter of the Sovereign Pontiff an important document to cite, to crown our study in its truth and greatness?

Do not these words of Pope Pius XII recall a part of the missionary history of the Sisters of Notre Dame, a history which Blessed Julie initiated, and then had the heroism to organize and to pursue, all of which we have related in a few pages, as a fruit of her spirituality?

One is impressed at once by the marvellous flowering of vocations and of schools, all due after God to her confidence in God, her love of Jesus Christ, her docility to the Holy Spirit, her Marian devotion.

For just as all the graces of the Holy Virgin in this world are the fruits of her co-redemption on Calvary, so the works, blessed by Providence, which the Sisters of Notre Dame have accomplished in the Universal Church have sprung from the dependent co-redemption of the Holy Virgin, from whom they acquired merits through a fervent fidelity to their spiritual life.

## A NOTE ON THE TYPE
## IN WHICH THIS BOOK IS SET

*This book is set in Fairfield, a Linotype face, created by Rudolph Ruzicka, distinguished American artist and engraver. Introduced in 1940, Fairfield is almost strictly a book type with much charm and beauty. It is easy to read as one learns from extensive reading since it furnishes some degree of stimulation and pleasure to the eye. The fitting of each letter is practically perfect, which is a real tribute to its designer. This book was composed by Progressive Typographers, Inc., of York, Pa., printed by the Wickersham Printing Company of Lancaster, Pa. and bound by Moore and Company of Baltimore, Md. The typography and design by Howard N. King.*